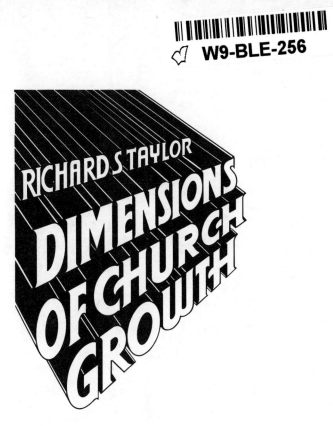

RICHARD S. TAYLOR

DIMENSIONS OF CHURCH GROWTH

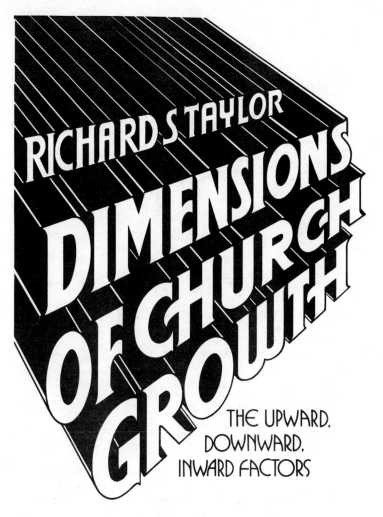

RICHARD S TAYLOR

DIMENSIONS OF CHURCH GROWTH

THE UPWARD,
DOWNWARD,
INWARD FACTORS

FOREWORD BY
WILLIAM GREATHOUSE

FRANCIS ASBURY PRESS
of Zondervan Publishing House
Grand Rapids, Michigan

Dimensions of Church Growth
Copyright © 1989 by Richard S. Taylor

Francis Asbury Press is an imprint of Zondervan Publishing House,
1415 Lake Drive, S.E., Grand Rapids, Michigan 49506.

Library of Congress Cataloging in Publication Data

Taylor, Richard Shelley
    Dimensions of church growth / Richard S. Taylor.
       p.   cm.
    Bibliography: p.
    ISBN 0-310-75411-9
    1. Church growth. I. Title.
BV652.25.T39   1989
254'.5–dc20
                                            89-16467
                                          CIP

Edited by Robert D. Wood

Printed in the United States of America

89 90 91 92 93 94 95 / PP / 10 9 8 7 6 5 4 3 2 1

CONTENTS

Part Two
OUTREACH DIMENSIONS

Part Three
DIMENSIONS IN NURTURING

FOREWORD

The name of Richard S. Taylor is loved and respected in contemporary Wesleyan holiness circles. Widely known as an instructive and convincing preacher of the Word, he is also recognized as a serious theologian and trenchant writer.

Drawing from his long experience as pastor, missionary, and seminary professor of theology and missions, Dr. Taylor develops a biblical theology and methodology of church growth that allows full play to the unique activity of the Holy Spirit and that perceives church growth in holistic terms rather than merely quantitative.

While he briefly discusses pros and cons of what he calls "Systems of Acceleration," such as telemarketing, he believes that the time-honored and proved community outreach through interpersonal contacts will build more solidly in the long run. Also, he stresses the importance of fostering spiritual renewal and of adopting methods that tend to turn "revivals" into *revival.*

However, Taylor devotes the final seven chapters of the book to methods of assimilating new converts, training and building them up in the faith, and the kind of pulpit instruction and pastoral counseling that will achieve the spiritual deepening and growth of a congregation. The three chapters on counseling are not only helpful but timely.

In laying his biblical and theological foundations, the author courageously points out what he views as inherent perils in the contemporary church growth movement. Those perils include the tendency to perceive church growth too lopsidedly in quantitative terms, with the inevitable one-sided emphasis on statistics. This issues in the multiplication of church activities designed to draw crowds, resulting almost inevitably in the substitution of human endeavor for the ministry of the Spirit, and depending more on systems and strategies than on the power of God.

A serious fallout from such intense concentration on statistical growth is the disposition to discount the traditional role of the pastor as shepherd of the flock of Christ. In scorning the "maintenance mentality," it is so easy to swing to the opposite pole of an aggressive expansionism tht skims over the pastoral care so essential to building up the body and its members. Caught in this mentality, the pastor is tempted to cut corners and compromise to see church growth, or, resisting this temptation, come under killing pressure and disabling guilt.

Admittedly, this book is controversial. However, it deserves a careful and thoughtful reading, particularly by the pastor whose heart yearns for authentic growth of his congregation in more than merely the numerical dimension.

In these eighteen chapters, Dr. Taylor "brings forth out of his treasure things new and old." He appropriates the best in both church-growth thought and pastoral theology, while drawing from his own rich experience and observation. I am happy to commend this book to all who work and pray to see Christ's church become truly "the seed of the kingdom" in our world.

William M. Greathouse

PREFACE

It is claimed that a palm tree will bend in a storm but will not fall because for every foot of height there is an equal foot of depth in the root system. A tree towering majestically one hundred feet is stabilized by a root that penetrates the earth one hundred feet.

This book is written for pastors who are as concerned about depth as they are about height in church growth. They are keenly aware that church growth is multidimensional. To think totally in terms of statistics is to think superficially. One is betrayed into methods of achieving statistics which not only sear one's own soul but produce a house of cards.

Yet the statistical dimension is not unimportant. It is not to be despised by an affectation of disdain for the "numbers game." Statistics mean people and people are souls for whom Christ died. A worthy pastor who loves Christ and people cannot be content with zero growth.

To aid pastors in this dimension of growth, I devote several chapters in this book to the methodology of outreach. Some of the newer methods are analyzed—with tips for success—but special stress is placed on the slower, more traditional method of growing a church in a community by growing roots and relationships in every direction. Some things are said also concerning the skills of personal evangelism.

But special stress also is placed on the importance of recovering the vision of revival. An entire chapter discusses the principles of promoting renewal, and we take a fresh look at the planned campaign in the local church. Also an attempt is made to incite faith for the great, sweeping moving of the Spirit which not only revolutionizes churches but cleanses whole communities. In our quest for new technologies we dare not permit ourselves to lose sight of the limitless power of the Holy Spirit—which, after all—is the unique mark of an authentic Christianity.

The foundational dimension, with which the book begins, is the biblical and theological. If this foundation is not solid in the pastor's own mind and in his methods, his work will be frothy and will not last. It will be "wood, hay, stubble" instead of "gold, silver, and precious stones," and will be consumed in the fires of judgment.

The lion's share of the book is devoted to the dimension of discipling. Getting people in is important, and difficult; but holding them and nurturing them into mature spiritual stature is far more difficult. This requires skills of a very high order. But it also requires time and patience. In our impatience we begrudge the time factor, and try to accelerate the nurturing process. The earlier chapter on parameters has something to say about this.

These chapters on nurturing seek to open up areas easily missed in the typical pulpit and classroom scope of subjects. Holiness of heart and life, the urgency and art of indoctrination, the training in ethics, spiritual formation, and the dynamics of growth are all areas that challenge the pastor's intellectual breadth and depth if he is going to lead his people beyond the shallows. Admittedly these chapters are "preachy," but my intention is to enlarge the pastor's understanding of the critical areas, and (I hope) to provide handles for transmitting these guidelines to his people.

Then follow three chapters on counseling. Certified

counselors may raise skeptical eyebrows and query, "Since when does a theologian know anything about counseling?" He knows enough to be afraid of counselors who are babes in theology! However, if a pastor's counseling is both pastoral and Christian (and how dare it be otherwise?), he will understand that counseling that is not informed biblically and theologically is not only missing the mark, but is a menace to the ministry.

The final chapter could have been this Preface. It reminds us of the power of the pastor. This power is incalculable. It is not authoritarian or political or juridical, but vastly exceeds any of these categories: it is moral and spiritual, and as such is the very underpinning of society.

I hope that this book will allay some needless stresses in the pastor's spirit, by helping him gain a more healthful concept of church growth. To this end a blunt diagnosis may be in order here.

The greatest hurdle for the typical pastor to get over is the frenzy for instant results which seems to be built into the contemporary mentality. We are a jumpy and jittery generation. If showy and glamorous results are not immediately forthcoming, we try something else or somewhere else—which may relate to the shamefully short pastorates we are now experiencing.

Though we may wince, let us not close our eyes to the truth: Too many pastors are marked by the mood of the day. They are long on vision but short on patience. They have been nurtured in a culture of immediacy. Through credit they have been able to possess *right now* what they have not yet earned. They have been encouraged by almost every shaping influence to gratify themselves today. They have sought out every possible shortcut through their education and training. Both temperamentally and culturally, therefore, they are ill-equipped for plodding, for waiting, for reverses, for detours, for deferred privilege and poky evidences of achievement. Yet these are the very capacities most fundamental to the pastorate.

Happy is the pastor who with a quiet spirit lives in the assurance of 1 Corinthians 15:58—"Therefore, my dear brothers, stand firm. Let nothing move you. Always give yourselves fully to the work of the Lord, because you know that your labor in the Lord is not in vain."

That's the best formula ever written for church growth!

Richard S. Taylor
Portland, Oregon
1989

ACKNOWLEDGMENTS

For their very helpful suggestions when they read the original manuscript of what has become two books, I am indebted to two veteran ministers, E. E. Zachary and P. J. Bartram. The first of these books is *Principles of Pastoral Success*. Now there is this one, *Dimensions of Church Growth*.

To Lyle Pointer and John Denney, successful pastors of the contemporary generation, I express my thanks for their candid and constructive criticism, which prompted some rewriting and more careful handling of certain issues.

To my district superintendent, Gerald E. Manker, I also owe a debt of gratitude for his warm encouragement following the reading of some portions to about twenty-five of his younger pastors. Superintendent Hugh Smith likewise responded to the original rough draft with an urging to see the project through to completion.

In addition, I owe a hearty thank you to Bob Wood whose skillful editing and wise counsel made this a better book.

1

OUR PERSPECTIVE—FROM ABOVE OR FROM BELOW?

O f recent years the emphases of personal evangelism, religious education, and such specialties as bus ministry have been overshadowed by the burgeoning, all-encompassing church growth movement. Beginning with Donald MaGavran's book, *How Churches Grow* (1959), and promoted by such authorities as C. Peter Wagner and Win Arne as well as MaGavran, the movement has mushroomed until it has become one of the dominant forces—if not *the* dominant force—in North American Protestantism.

The premise of the movement is that the local church is the visible locus of the kingdom of God, and that the kingdom is extended most normatively by the growth of churches and the planting of new churches. The church, it is believed, is intended by God to be the hub of evangelism and missions, and the cradle of Christian nurture. It is in the church that Christians find their true identity. In the church they find the indispensable elements of growth and service—fellowship, discipline, instruction, corporate worship, and cooperative ways for fulfilling the Great Commission. Evangelism is not complete until converts are brought into the church. Elementary to Christian growth is churchmanship.

It is believed that new converts cannot learn to function as healthy, biblical Christians except within a local body of believers. Religious mavericks become spiritually dwarfed and often twisted in notions and perceptions. Obviously, religious lone wolves can seldom accomplish on their own what is possible as a disciplined member of a church family.

Parachurch movements have unique forms of ministry, which transcend denominational lines. But their strength is largely drawn from the churches. And they relate to the churches as feeders or bleeders. If they are bleeders the good they do is at least partially dissipated by their undermining effect on the churches.

The church growth movement has produced a vast amount of literature, growing out of extensive research into the sociology, demographics, and psychology of church growth. Great acumen has been shown in tracing the flow lines of development, and pointing out the milieus and conditions in which church growth has occurred, and in which further growth seems most likely. Some environments are seen as conducive to growth and others are seen as inhibitive.

To foster church growth a literature has developed aimed at retraining pastors to think in church-growth terms, and to become goal-oriented. Correlating with this is the simultaneous education in retraining the laity to turn from their inwardness to think growth. This has led to totally new methodologies in organization and style, including the adoption of Madison Avenue sales principles, more effective advertising, and even telemarketing.

To the extent that church growth consists of the true extension of the kingdom of the Lord Jesus Christ, defined in terms of sinners being born again and assimilated into the life of the body by the Holy Spirit, the movement is a twentieth-century phenomenon whose time has come and for which we should praise God. It can be an activity of total evangelism focused where it should be focused, in the local church both as an organization and as an organism.

But the movement has inherent perils which thoughtful persons are beginning to see. It is easy to think quantitatively, and see church growth too one-sidedly in terms of statistics. Statistical gains can become a mirage which appears real but vanishes upon close inspection. It can be almost totally an external multiplication of activities and the gathering of crowds, which in the end immunizes participants from the profound changes that vital Christianity offers and demands. People can be swept along by an endless plethora of exciting church activities: athletics, social services, musicals, competitions, celebrity personalities, choirs, retreats, emotionally moving services—all spiced with happy camaraderie and fun, yet through it all never getting to the heart of things with God.

The responsible leaders of the church growth movement have sought to avoid this by urging prayer and stressing the ministry of the Spirit. But their good intentions notwithstanding, the primary attention has been devoted to finding and developing systems and strategies. In the process, the drift has been toward a humanistic framework of ideas. And too often in actual fact the principles of prayer and Spirit-power have been rendered lip service more than resorted to as the underpinnings of everything that is done.

There are several possible negative fallouts to the intense concentration on church growth that has gripped pastors and their leaders.

One is the disposition to discount the traditional role

of the pastor as a shepherd. Considerable scorn has been heaped upon the "maintenance" mentality. Of course there is need for a corrective here, for many have been content, as congregations and pastors, to drift in a comfortable and amiable coziness as a static church family, with little passion for the lost around them. But it is easy for the pendulum of our value systems to swing from the comfortable church family appeal to a kind of aggressive expansionism that skims over the intimate attachments and slow rooting of spiritual faith that is essential for church durability and richness. It becomes too easy for eager, ambitious, young pastors to mistake their ambition for soul passion, and to evaluate a church in terms of its church-growth potential, with the philosophy—even occasionally voiced aloud—that they want to see possibilities for *doing* something, by which they mean something numerically explosive. They want not just a crowd but crowds, and they scorn the idea of simply ministering to a church that shows no immediate promise of bursting at the seams.

The thrill and satisfaction of being a shepherd has not gripped these pastors. They do not revel in the privilege of teaching the young, ministering to the sick and aged, marrying the living and burying the dead, discipling converts in slow, unglamorous ways, indoctrinating a whole generation, nurturing them to sturdy spiritual adulthood, spending hours in prayer and in their studies to dig out the meat of the Word that they might feed hungry worshipers year after year by solid, constructive preaching. That is too tame and stolid and slow-paced for them. Their ideal is the ballyhooed church which moved from 17 members to 2000 in two years. In their minds unless something like that is happening, nothing worthwhile is going on. This sort of thing is their measure of success and their consuming drive. To this end they will push their church, and if it does not quickly respond to the big-time dimensions, they will look elsewhere for a more "promising" opportunity (as they define the term).

To the extent that the church-growth motif has fed this kind of pastoral temperament, to that extent the movement has become a mania—church growth as an end in itself—and in the long run will self-destruct. It seems to the beginner to be the shortest route to the ecclesiastical top. This syncs with the temperament of the baby-boomer generation, which has little patience for slow processes and small appreciation for roots. Action is the demand, visible, palpable, measurable action. This is the American mood, perhaps more today than ever in our history.

A further side effect has been the creation of killing pressure in the parsonage. Not all preachers, young or old, have the temperament or ability to be highly successful church-growth pastors. But the clamor for church growth, heard everywhere, has imposed on them the pressure of oughtness and the desperation of finding ways of producing it or risk being passed by in the pastoral game of musical chairs. They therefore live harried lives and carry disabling guilt because in spite of all they do their statistics are not very impressive when the annual church conference or assembly focuses the relentless eyes of leaders and peers and laypersons upon them.

The result of church-growth pressure has too often resulted in perspectives which are more from below than from above. It is time we look up and begin to see our task from God's standpoint rather than from that of ecclesiastical superiors.

It may seem presumptuous to suggest God's standpoint, but I will attempt to nevertheless.

First, I must drive a preliminary nail. The pastoral role in the New Testament is primarily shepherding, only secondarily evangelizing. True, Paul said to Timothy, "Do the work of an evangelist," but the reading of Paul's two epistles to this young pastor will reveal the real center of emphasis—Timothy's pastoral task. In the list of God's gifts to the church, the function of pastor/teacher is distinct from the calling of the evangelist (Eph. 4:11). Jesus said to Peter, "Feed my sheep." It was this assignment which stuck most of all in Peter's mind so that years later he could say, "Be shepherds of God's flock that is under your care" (1 Peter 5:2).

Rare is the man or woman who is gifted both as a shepherd and an evangelist. Generally one function will be done well, but at the expense of the other. A pastor who can bring people in and reach them for Christ had better build a staff of shepherds. A pastor who can shepherd well would be wise to utilize extensively the aid of able evangelists, both on his staff, and in special revival campaigns. A church nurtured totally on outreach will become intellectually and spiritually shallow and vulnerable to the perils of excessive excitement and emotionalism. Yet it is equally true that a total concentration on doctrine and instruction will produce truth-hardened Pharisees if there is no flow-through to the world around.

But we reaffirm the thesis: A man or woman entering the pastoral ministry should learn—and be taught at seminary or Bible college—to see his task first of all as shepherding. Let him study the art of shepherding. The ideal is both shepherding and growing. But too often these days we are witnessing the sorry spectacle of all the eggs being put into the church-growth basket, the pastor thinking of nothing else with the result that the sheep whom God entrusted to his care are neglected, hungry, and bedraggled. And wandering off in .droves.

Next, a new examination of the theology of church growth may bring a breath of fresh air to our souls. We will make this examination in the next five chapters. We will discover that we are instruments in God's hands, not primarily His agents. Therefore, ours is to invest our energies; it is His to keep the records.[1]

Third, we will see that the most important thing pastors can do to assure success is to be the kind of persons God can trust and work through. This requires pure motives, genuine love, irreproachable ethics, a humble, Christlike spirit, spiritual and intellectual depth, and a character that is durable.

The pastor who will succeed in God's eyes must be moved by what moves God. What moves God is the sight of humanity trapped in sin and hurtling toward a devil's hell. It is doubtful that comparative statistics between this or that church, or this or that conference, or rewards for so-called evangelistic achievement move God very much. His reaction may rather be tolerant amusement over the humanity of His children. But He will give Himself to that man or woman who sees people through God's eyes, and who shares the same compassion and drive which Paul testified to when he said, "Christ's love compels us" (2 Cor. 5:14). Such a pastor will operate on a higher level than motives that look to the awards of men or measure ministry by size or quantity. He will want crowds because he wants to reach more people for Christ, not because he desires commendation for being able to report church growth.

We dare not mince words here. What is being declared is that it is terribly easy for pastors to be driven by expectations from below rather than animated by drawings and energizing from above. If from below, schemes will be devised to achieve purely statistical goals. If from above, the leadership of the Spirit will be sought in fulfilling God's will in this place. God's will includes evangelism, but it also includes patient nurturing and teaching, line upon line and precept upon precept, without one eye being cocked too nervously on the statistical chart and the looming annual report.

Pastors need emancipation, not from soul burden or hard labor, but from the stress of man-made expectations. At some point, therefore, while they neither despise nor ignore denominational goals, they must get themselves and those goals "on the altar" so that they can work in inner freedom from anxiety. Ultimately, they are answerable to God, not to man, even human leaders; and this responsibility to God must control their motivation, their methodology, and their emotional state.

It is to be feared that the "death to self" preached to laymen is sometimes missed by preachers. An altar needs to be found somewhere at which the questions of goals, human expectations, church size, and even church growth (as an end in itself) are settled once for all, so profoundly that the pastor will never feel driven again by the crack of someone else's whip. This Waterloo to the old self must include the entire issue of bigness versus smallness. A pastor who cannot serve a small church to the glory of God would not be able to glorify God in a big church.

A former seminary student of mine was reluctantly preparing for the ministry. Inwardly he wished he could find a way out. During part of his student days his voice gave him trouble, and I suspected that he hoped for a welcome escape through the avenue of that problem. He successfully sold cars on the side and the business world appealed to him. But at the beginning of his last semester he had a session with the Lord in his kitchen one morning. He "had it out." In the process he surrendered completely to God's total will for his life, was cleansed of his doublemindedness, and filled with the Holy Spirit. From that moment he thought of nothing but entering the ministry.

During that spring semester church after church was offered to him by eager district superintendents, including some very good churches. Each time when he prayed he got a no answer from the Lord. Finally one superintendent, in exasperation, said, "It looks to me as if you just want to spend your life in Podunk Center." "That will be fine with me," was the answer, "if that is what the Lord wants." Finally a church was offered which no one else wanted. The building was run-down, bills were piling up, the small group of people was discouraged, and it was in a sleepy prairie town—about as unpromising, unglamorous, and unexciting as could be imagined. Gung-ho, ambitious, "let-me-at-'em" theologues who hadn't done similar business with God would not have given it a second look. But when this young man prayed, the Lord said, "This is it" and he took it. Little could he have foreseen that within a few years, through a series of unexpected developments, that sleepy little town would become a growing, thriving, bursting-at-the-seams college town, and he would be preaching to some 1,500 people every Sunday morning in a multi-million dollar sanctuary.

But we must not miss the point. If the Lord had revealed this to him in advance, and said, "If you will take this little church that no one else wants, I'll turn it into one of the largest churches in the denomination," a *real death to self would have been psychologically impossible.* That knowledge had to be withheld from him. True death to selfish ambition can be experienced only on the basis of the worst possible scenario, sincerely expected and totally accepted. Knowing the man, I believe he would have been faithful and obedient even if the church had remained relatively small and the little town sleepy.

So becoming usable is our primary obligation. Church growth for church growth's sake must be surrendered, just as all other criteria for success as success is measured among men. Then God can help us grow a church in its total dimensions, calmly and without panic or haste or compromise, not only quantitative but qualitative, not only size but depth.

2

THEOLOGICAL FOUNDATIONS

It hardly needs to be argued that "church growth" not theologically grounded is not the growth of the church but something else. But if so grounded, there will be several biblical foundation stones underlying all methodology.

1. *God has already declared His desire and provision to save all people.* This breath-taking affirmation is in the Bible's best known verse: "For God so loved the world that he gave his one and only Son, that whoever believes in him shall not perish but have eternal life" (John 3:16). This is reaffirmed by Paul: "This is good, and pleases God our Savior, who wants all men to be saved and to come to a knowledge of the truth" (1 Tim. 2:3). Peter says the same thing: "The Lord . . . is patient with you, not wanting anyone to perish, but everyone to come to repentance" (2 Peter 3:9). This means that God wants us to reach more and more people. He does not want to see a single empty pew in our sanctuary. He desires that our outreach extend to the last unsaved person in our community; or, on the missionary level, in our world. God is *for* church growth!

Our intercessory praying has been ordained by God as a link in the chain of divine method, but it should not be viewed as a means of persuading God to become interested in the people we are trying to reach. It is His prior interest which has created ours. If our concern in prayer is not purely the echo of His, then it is prompted by other than His motives. Perhaps all unconsciously we are striving in prayer for people that we might build *our* church.

2. *Christ has already claimed responsibility for church growth.* "I will build my church," He declares (Matt. 16:18). If what is built is the pastor's and not Christ's, then the product may be religious and it may be exciting, but it is not Christ's church.

Christ will build His church with or without this or that pastor. If God can use him, He will. But if there are elements in his motives or in his spirit or in his life which make him unusable, God will set him aside and work through someone else. This applies not only to men but to movements and denominations as well. When God no longer has total control, when mere size becomes an end in itself, when the entity becomes a self-perpetuating institution instead of an instrument, or when self-aggrandizement and empire-building and dynasty-establishing take over, God just tacks on the door "Ichabod" and moves on to a channel He can work through. For it is Christ's church, not ours; and Christ will not surrender or even share His prerogatives as its builder. We must learn to be *His* humble and obedient instruments and stop trying to harness His power as *our* Celestial Expeditor.

3. *Christ's appointed method is Pentecost.* There are humanistic ways a congregation can be gathered and multifaceted programs put in place that only simulate the true church. An authentic church growth must be the

work of the Holy Spirit through Spirit-filled men and women.

Without Pentecost the religion of Jesus Christ would either have vaporized in the first generation, or shriveled into an impotent sect of Judaism. It was only when the apostles were filled with the Spirit that they ceased being obstacles and began to be instruments. Self was out of the way. Their preoccupation with rivalry and position was at an end. A new kind of power possessed them because it could now flow through clean channels. The result was continuous revival with rapid expansion, even in the face of cruel persecution.

Pentecost is still God's method, and it is the rankest of follies to presume to substitute methods of our own. While the Day of Pentecost as a moment in history, with its unique inaugural signs, cannot be repeated, its lasting essentials must continue to be experienced—fullness, purity, and power, in and through the immediate, personal, controlling presence of the Holy Spirit.

Ours is a supernatural religion from beginning to end or it is a fraud. Our methods must be shaped by total reliance on the Spirit and profound faith in what He can do. I once heard a church leader tell pastors, "God can't fill your church." That is the language of unbelief. While God probably will not fill the churches of lazy or unworthy pastors, He can do what in His sovereignty He chooses to do. The history of revivals is full of demonstrations of God's ability to fill churches virtually overnight.[1] What can be conceded is that the Spirit's usual mode of building Christ's church is more slowly paced, stone upon stone and block upon block (1 Peter 2:5); or as a body grows (Eph. 4:16).

The centrality of the Spirit as God's method for church growth has its corollaries. One is a new dependence on prayer. Pentecost was the climax of a ten-day prayer meeting. Thereafter the church proceeded on its knees. In the book of Acts, prayer is seen as the day-by-day operational procedure. It was the frequent and unfailing recourse of the apostolic church. When threatened they did not call a committee meeting to plan strategy; they called a prayer meeting (Acts 4). The disciples had marveled at their Lord's prayer life, and once said, "Teach us to pray"; but in spite of this request, there is little evidence that prayer was very meaningful in their personal lives until Pentecost, when suddenly they were attuned to prayer because they were Spirit-filled. Prayer moved from a mere desire to center stage.

4. *Our hope of success is in the knowledge that the Spirit is already at work.* "When he comes," Jesus promised, "he will convict the world of guilt in regard to sin and righteousness and judgment" (+1John 16:8). This convicting ministry is going on even before we reach people. When we evangelize one-on-one, the Holy Spirit has gone ahead of us, is working with us, and will follow up after we have left. Some may have resisted and become hard, but their hardness is not because the Spirit has passed them by. Others may also resist our efforts, but their resistance will not be due to a failure of the Spirit to probe and move them even while we speak. It will be due to the person's free choice. While the Spirit's convicting power is unavoidable, it is not irresistible.

Unless blocked by sin, heresy, or unbelief in us, we can be sure that our public evangelism is accompanied by the immediate action of the Holy Spirit on the audience. The intensity of this action will greatly vary in degree, but the action may be counted on. The Spirit honors Christ when He is presented and the Word when it is preached. The preacher may not feel this power; in fact, he may feel like a pulpit orphan. He may feel utterly impotent in his struggle to communicate, yet all the while the truth may be finding its mark. The Spirit will always be working, if given the components of purity, obedience, prayer, faith, and truth.[2] It will bear repeating again and again: Expansion of a congregation that can be achieved by humanistic methods on their own is something other than "church" growth in God's sight. If the Spirit hasn't done it, it is counterfeit.

5. *The prescribed* modus operandi *has already been made known: spreading the Word by witnessing, preaching, and teaching in every language, with our ministry supported by holy living and good works.* The form includes both the written word and the spoken word. While Pentecost is God's primary method for reaching the lost, at its heart is this operational method of verbal communication.

"Jews demand miraculous signs and Greeks look for wisdom, but we preach Christ crucified," declares Paul (1 Cor. 1:22–23). The first fruit of Pentecost resulted from a sermon. Ours is a speaking religion. It is the method of communicating the gospel with the objective of persuading people to accept and act upon it.

Any form of coercion is unbiblical, for it violates the freedom that must mark a personal relationship with God. Human personhood must be respected at all times. God does and therefore so must His representatives. Only as people freely choose to believe and obey does their religious faith have either authenticity or moral value. The church has always violated its own character and shamed its Lord when it has resorted to forms of compulsion. This is the sure mark of cultism and heresy.

The premise that God's method is communication with a view to persuasion has within it a stern implication. It is that the tendency in some quarters to denigrate preaching is unbiblical. Preaching is not an ego trip. It is not a brash arrogation of religious authority that presumes to tell people how to manage their lives. Preaching is rather an act of obedience to Almighty God, who has acted in Christ on our behalf and commissioned chosen servants to be His heralds. "All this is from God," writes Paul, "who reconciled us to himself through Christ and gave us the ministry of reconciliation" (2 Cor. 5:18). The preacher's holy and wonderful calling is to say, "We implore you on Christ's behalf: Be reconciled to God" (v. 20b). What Paul writes to Pastor Timothy, God says to every other pastor: "Preach the Word" (2 Tim. 4:2).

6. *Church growth must be defined in terms of the new birth.* Due to the legal and physical complexities of our age, formal membership in a local church has now become a usual procedure. But church growth cannot properly be defined simply in terms of the accession of new members. This is to turn the correct order on its head. The Word speaks significantly in the simple summary: "The Lord added to their number daily those who were being saved" (Acts 2:47b). "Being saved" must be permitted to carry its full weight of meaning. They were being inducted into Christ. They were experiencing everything Jesus meant by the expressions "born again" and "born of the Spirit" (+ 1John 3:3, 7–8). For them this involved repentance, public baptism in the name of Jesus, and the forgiveness of sins (Acts 2:38). Furthermore, it involved a commitment to obey Peter's command, "Save yourselves from this corrupt generation" (v. 40): in other words, a complete break with the world, including apostate religion.

The statement that "the Lord was adding to their number" means that Christ through His Spirit was drawing each convert into the fellowship of the body and inwardly conforming him to it. He sensed family. He belonged. He knew he belonged and other believers knew he belonged. In our day he would have "joined" formally; but if valid, the public joining would have been only a public acknowledgment of the spiritual union which had already occurred.

Should we not allow this basic truth to temper our lust for joiners, and to preserve in our minds a biblical perspective on church growth? Even in the early church there doubtless were camp followers—persons who hung around the assembly of believers, and at times were mistaken for them. But unless in *God's sight* they had been "saved," they were not in *God's sight* in the church. God does not add unregenerate persons to the fellowship. God sees church growth not in the increase of countable bodies but in the increase of those being saved, and whose relation to the church is solidly grounded on being saved.

If therefore we are going to work with God as His instruments, we had better make every effort to make sure that those we take in as members are being added by God. Otherwise what we call the church will deviate further and further from God's approval. What is the value of "church growth" if what we are "growing" is something other than what God identifies as the church? We should take very seriously the biblical distinction between building with "wood, hay or straw" as against "gold, silver, costly stones" (1 Cor. 3:11–15).

All of which reminds us that the church is not a field for evangelism. We reverse the divine order and bring upon ourselves multiplied debacles and disasters when we gather people into church membership on the assumption that we will get them saved later. They will destroy the church rather. Being unregenerate they could not do otherwise, no matter how well intentioned they might be as persons. "The man without the Spirit does not accept the things that come from the Spirit of God, for they are foolishness to him, and he cannot understand them, because they are spiritually discerned" (1 Cor. 2:14).

7. *The prescribed method prohibits racism, parochialism,*

and provincialism. Central to any discussion of the theology of church growth must be the Great Commission. To abandon the missionary emphasis is already to have abandoned God's prescribed course for His church, and to doom the church to atrophy. For the church is more than a local body of believers; it is the body of God's people everywhere. A pastor's necessary commitment to his particular flock may tend, if he is not watchful, to result in tunnel vision, by which he sees nothing beyond his flock. He becomes indifferent to the church across town, and even more seriously, indifferent to the cutting edge of evangelism on the other side of the world. The pastor who has a proper church-growth vision will avoid parochialism and maintain the broad view, which means that in building his own congregation he will be continuously building into them a world vision. While a pastor may feel that he is carrying out the Great Commission by fulfilling it in his particular corner, he will become small-souled, and his people will become small-souled, if he does not, while reaching people at home, keep his and their eyes on the fields abroad.

History shows that there is no better way to assure growth and prosperity at home than to develop a strong missionary-mindedness. Money given to missions and prayer time spent for missions always seems to double back in blessing to the local church.

3

THE QUESTION OF AUXILIARY METHODS

At this point we need an eighth proposition in our theological summary: *The Spirit desires to guide pastors in their search for specific methods.* This returns us to the question of strategies and their legitimacy. We began with a warning against a human-oriented perspective of church growth, and we sought to show that church growth begins with God. God is *for* church growth and has made available through the Spirit all necessary resources for its achievement. Where then does human strategy fit into the scenario? To what extent is it consistent with the spiritual nature of our mission to utilize purely secular bait? To what extent are we to reach people by moving them into the sphere of the church's influence by indirect stages—appealing to something they are interested in, such as church athletics, in order to win them to Christ?

THE EARLY CHURCH IDEAL

Let us look briefly at the utter simplicity of the early church in Jerusalem. The church devised no programs.

They called no conferences to invent organizational structures for the purpose of improving their evangelizing techniques. The apostles preached and taught daily, the believers listened and practiced. Church life was fervent yet uncomplicated: "They devoted themselves to the apostles' teaching and to the fellowship, to the breaking of bread and to prayer" (Acts 2:42). The bread-breaking and eating took place in each other's homes as well as in more public places. Their exuberant joy, obvious love for one another, and their unmistakable discovery of something wonderful brought them into "the favor of all the people" (v. 47).

Therefore, we may say that the rapid growth of the church in those early days was traceable to four factors:

a. The initial surge of pentecostal power was still flowing, and the Spirit was moving not only in anointing the speakers but by supporting signs and wonders—of which the book of Acts is full.

b. The behavior and radiant faces of the Christians were convincing to the observing populace. This made a profound impact.

c. The gospel seed was falling on ready soil. After all, the residents of Jerusalem were for the most part Jews, profoundly religious, and strong believers in a coming Messiah. Many had seen and heard Jesus and could not escape His pull on their hearts. In spite therefore of the bitter opposition of the Sanhedrin, the mass of people, including many priests, were highly receptive (Acts 6:7).

d. The church was aggressive in its evangelism. "Day after day, in the temple courts and from house to house, they never stopped teaching and proclaiming the good news that Jesus is the Christ" (Acts 5:42).

This is still the ideal formula for rapid church growth. For reasons not understood, populations in different parts of the world have been peculiarly prepared by God, even without the advantages which the Jews had. When reached by the gospel the flow of grace seemed to pour in to fill the hungry void, with mass movements resulting.

It is when pentecostal fires smolder that the church has to cast about for novel methods to compensate for its own spiritual loss. Then come the programs, schemes, gimmicks, and manipulations to gather a few stray converts. And the problem is compounded manyfold when the church seeks to evangelize, as today, in an environment that too often is either hostile or indifferent. So it becomes a scramble to find ways to *get attention,* for the church believes that if only the unchurched can be brought into the sphere of the church's influence many will find the Lord. While the contemporary church has all the resources of Pentecost available, it seems, too often, to have forgotten how to utilize them. Therefore, it feverishly resorts to secular props.

But the answer is still revival. The pastor and church that will pay the price for precipitating revival in first-century proportions will obtain first-century results. And in some places exactly this is being done.

PAUL'S "ALL THINGS"

We have come full circle. While praying for revival and seeking to keep in step with the Spirit, are there strategies which the Lord would be pleased to have the church use and which He can bless to make a difference? Strategies which can be learned from society and which may have the smell of the secular world on them?

A biblical basis for a possible answer is Paul's

strategic principle: "I have become all things to all men so that by all possible means I might save some" (1 Cor. 9:22b). The context shows that this strategy is twofold: First he seeks to *serve* all in order to win some; second, he identifies himself with the group he is with in order to win them—to the Jew he finds common ground with them as a Jew, whereas to the Gentile he seeks the common ground of freedom from the Mosaic Law. He adapts himself to the person or group he is working with. Yet he is not a chameleon, for there is no compromise in his moral principles or changeableness in his fundamental objectives. He does not participate in the errors or sins of others as an evangelistic strategy. He does, however, stand with them at the point of their need and their understanding and seeks to lead them from that point. His identification is such that they sense a bond with him. He is constantly seeking bridges of communication and community, which will provide access to their hearts. He refuses to hide behind unnecessary barriers, but seeks their removal whenever possible without compromise.

If Paul were pastoring today, would he haunt hospital corridors not just to minister but to win people? Would he knock on doors? Would he advertise? An affirmative answer carries a high level of probability. We already know by his own testimony that he taught them not only publicly but from "house to house" (Acts 20:20). But would he in addition utilize church athletics, dinners, concerts, service club activity as soul-winning strategy? Here we are not on sure ground. We know that he would major on prayer, person-to-person evangelism, and preaching (probably fiery!). But the extent to which he would resort to *attention-getting devices*—bait to get folks within his reach—is a debatable question. His "by all means" principle would suggest that he would stop at nothing that he thought would work so long as the Spirit endorsed it and it did not cheapen his cause. That, he would believe, would be counterproductive.

Paul certainly would seek to protect the sanctity of Christ's name and the dignity of the church. Some strategies are Madison Avenue-born not altar-born. Gimmicks that are perceived as gimmicks by the sophisticated create an impression of deception. It is doubtful therefore if Paul would resort to subterfuges as evangelistic strategy. While he would utilize honorable and honest means of getting attention and bringing people into the sphere of friendship, he would not use ruses that might appear to be tricky or deceptive. His flat denial of such methods is clear enough (1 Thess. 2:3).

Perhaps the sum of the matter is that since there are barriers between the unsaved and the church, barriers of prejudice, misunderstanding, fear, and indifference, it is not only legitimate but obligatory to seek very human ways of removing these barriers. To put it differently: a deep psychological and spiritual chasm separates the world from the church. While the Spirit is already striving out there, it is consistent with the Spirit's ministry—and the Great Commission—for the church to seek ways to build bridges across this chasm. The fundamental bridge must be love, but love *manifested* in friendship, neighborliness, helpfulness, and genuine involvement. This may include playing together as a beginning. When we have played with people, it will be easier to pray with them. Hence a modest, carefully controlled athletic program could conceivably be an evangelistic net by which Christians become "fishers of men." The danger would be in permitting such secondary activities to become the tail that wags the dog.

As for organization, per se, the early church organized as need arose. The very multiplication of numbers (Acts 6:1) made it impossible to carry on in the simple way that at first was adequate. An acute problem arose that was managerial in nature. In response the first "board of deacons" was established. But *multiplication produced the organization; organization did not produce the multiplication.* It never has and never will. At the most, it can provide a frame for Spirit-motivated activity and contribute to operational efficiency and internal harmony. Pipes help water reach the point of need; pipes do not create the water. Organization is needed to channel spiritual power, but organization cannot create spiritual power. The prayer closet is the source for that.

4

THE PASTOR AS AGENT

O ur theology of evangelistic dynamics needs to be pursued more minutely. What is the relation of the human to the divine? In doing the Lord's work, does the initiative respecting methodology rest with man or with the Holy Spirit? That the Holy Spirit is the worker's source of power is universally recognized among evangelicals. Not only does He endue the worker but effects the results. How, then, can the exact relationship of the pastor to the Holy Spirit be spelled out? What are the respective roles, and how do these roles function? An examination of two possible models may prove helpful. The first is to view the pastor as agent.

In this model the pastor is seen as the change agent who takes the initiative in devising methods and plans, but depends on the Spirit to endorse the plans and endue them with divine energy. Pastors who thus perceive their role might claim for themselves David's prayer: "May he give you the desire of your heart and make all your plans succeed" (Ps. 20:4).

SOME BIBLICAL POINTERS

There are at least three strong biblical pointers favoring this model. One is the biblical concept of stewardship. While the Bible at times sees a master or owner as a hands-on manager, it also commonly suggests a stewardship possessing considerable autonomy. The typical steward is largely on his own. He is given areas of responsibility or a specific job to do, then allowed wide latitude in devising ways and means as, for instance, in the Parable of the Talents (Matt. 25:14–20).

The validity of this model can be further argued from the Great Commission and the outpouring of the Spirit on the Day of Pentecost.

The church *has* its commission. It is told to go into all the world preaching the gospel and making disciples. This commission authenticates the outreach ministry of the local church. By winning people and growing, the local church is simply obeying God. Obviously this does not need a special revelation or prayer meeting for authorization. The pastor and local church have a stewardship, and their job is to find the best ways to fulfill it.

Neither (following this line of reasoning) does the church need to fast and pray for the presence and activity of the Holy Spirit. He has been given to the church and to the world. The Day of Pentecost marked the advent of the dispensation of the Holy Spirit. Jesus promised that He could be depended upon to convict the world of sin, righteousness, and judgment, and to empower the preaching of the gospel. Since this is the case, the pastor as an agent can be sure that if he invents and implements wise plans, God will give him the results.

The imagery here suggests the Spirit's activity as a wind that is already and always blowing redemptively. The human agent's task is to erect sails to the wind in the form of strategies and plans. The better the plan the larger the sail will prove to be, resulting in harnessing a larger measure of divine power for the propulsion of the ship of evangelism. Plans without the dynamic of the winds of the Spirit will prove useless, while the winds of the Spirit cannot accomplish their aims without the erection of sails.

A THEOLOGICAL CLUE

Further support for seeing the pastor as agent is to be found in Arminian theology, which affirms that the number who will respond is not predetermined by divine decree. If such were the case, the number would be limited by that decree, and no amount of doubling or tripling evangelistic saturation would alter it. But the responsibility resting on pastor and people burgeons if the eternal result is determined not by divine decree but in real measure by the efforts of the churches. The assumption of Arminianism is that people are free to accept or reject the gospel, undetermined by prior decree; and that in their freedom they are susceptible, not only to the influences of the Spirit, but to the influences of evangelistic enterprises. A sermon, a song, a simple invitation, a show of love, the hand of friendship—any one or a combination or these small events may tip the scales in influencing personal decision for Christ.

A church in Oregon hosted 206 needy people from the community to a free turkey dinner during the Christmas season of 1988. Four of the families served attended church services the following Sunday and one of the families accepted Christ. Arminian theology says that this was not a package of events predetermined by divine decree and therefore inevitable, but an association of actions linking voluntary service with voluntary and optional response. Of course the Holy Spirit worked through the service and upon the families, but His action, while an indispensable factor in the net of influences, did not "fix" the outcome.

SOME SOBERING IMPLICATIONS

The division of labor is on this model quite simple. The plans are human, the power is divine. The pastor thinks and schemes and studies to put plans and systems in place, and if they are essentially biblical (an important assumption), he may be sure that the Spirit will prosper them. But this does not release the pastor from anxiety, for the responsibility for devising the right plans and methods rests upon his shoulders, and poor plans or languid effort will mean fewer converts.

This is the model assumed by much contemporary literature on church growth. "Get a vision," counsels one church leader. "Then put into place a system which will assure the realization of the vision." The right systems, designed for specific church goals, will guarantee the particular results wished for. If these results are not realized, either the system was wrong or its implementation was inept.

The wisdom of the plans, on this basis, will be determined by the human understanding invested in them. Two assumptions are borrowed from the world. The first is the assumption of a law of averages—that is, that a percentage of people will respond to advertising, and that the response will be just about in direct proportion to the amount of advertising. One life insurance salesman started out every morning with one hundred business cards, and simply knocked on doors— cold turkey—until he got rid of every card. He knew that out of one hundred contacts some would be interested and phone back. If he could have distributed two hundred in a day his sales would have increased proportionately. This was the philosophy on which he operated at least five days a week, and he was successful.

The pastor who operates on such a hypothesis believes that a certain percentage of the people "out there" are already being especially moved upon by the Holy Spirit. They are already hungry and receptive. If he can just get the attention of a large enough number of people he is bound to catch in his net some of these ready folk. Therefore, he designs systems and plans that will enable him to capture the attention not of a few but hundreds, even thousands. He schemes to put into place a large net.

Of course personal free will responds or rejects the church's overtures and thus becomes the final determiner. But if the hypothesis noted above is correct—that a proportion of the people are open to persuasion—then the responsibility resting on pastors and their churches becomes almost unbearable. No room is left for a lukewarm approach to the task of soul winning. The conclusion is that improved methods simply mean more people won to Christ and saved for heaven. A cavalier approach to evangelism spells the doom of many who will not be reached by such a half-hearted approach. If our systems are too porous, many will slip through who might have been caught by a tighter net.

This hypothesis is undoubtedly sound. The pastor in his labor and planning should keep it always in mind. Because of this degree of hunger "out there" the right efforts on his part cannot totally be fruitless.

The second assumption needs careful scrutiny. It is the assumption that the church tends to borrow from the world, that "selling" is entirely a matter of using the right psychology. When the church unconsciously imbibes this premise it begins a subtle drift toward humanism. The supposition is adopted that the same attention-getting devices which the world of Madison Avenue employs will work equally well for the church.

Madison Avenue knows that certain stimuli get attention. Certain things appeal, others turn people off. Certain motifs create feelings of desire, others repel. Certain signals influence people to act; others do not. The world, working with the tools of psychology and technology, can virtually assure the success of any product or project. The world has learned the art of devising the catchy slogans and captions; the art of appealing to vanity and self-interest; the skillful use of color, sound, motion, surprise, and when possible even smell; the use of sex appeal in all possible forms; repetitive advertising—getting the message out in explosive, attention-grabbing, eye-riveting, and mouth-watering flair combined with overwhelming saturation. The potential market is literally blanketed with continuous assault. The belief on which the secular world operates is that even if the populace does not initially want the product, they can be made to want it, then made to feel they must have it.

When this principle of sales psychology is borrowed by the church, we come to believe that since we already have the best product in the world, our sole task is selling it. And if Madison Avenue methods will work for the world, they will work for us. Therefore, success in evangelizing and church growing is entirely a matter of getting into place the right selling and delivery system.

But not all is gold that glitters. A second look will disclose the fallacy of adopting the world's methodology wholesale. While we should try not to be Exhibit A of Jesus' dictum, that the world is wiser in its generation than the children of light, we must not simply echo the world, but realize fully that the world's motifs are not ours. The world appeals to the public's prurient, selfish, and professional interests. Advertising is controlled by motifs of vanity, pleasure, sex, power, possessions. These appeals are powerful because in fallen human nature these are the prized values.

Does the church unconsciously develop kinds of appeal which basically are the same—pleasure, excitement, happiness, self-esteem, being somebody special, success, positive thinking, "you can do anything you want to do"? And so the evangelistic pitch is that whatever the world is offering you can find in Christ, only better. But the church at this point had better be honest, and say that what God requires is repentance, surrender, obedience, and holiness. Suddenly the bait will lose its allure.

It will be appealing only to those who have been made sick of the world's bait, and are looking for something not just the same but radically higher and different. This will not be the mass of people aimed at by Madison Avenue. It will be a tiny minority. While it is true that the goods the church offers include peace of mind and inner happiness, that prospect is hidden by the biblical, totally unpsychological order of appeal: "Repent ye, and believe the gospel" (Mark 1:15, KJV). The gospel is good news to those willing to repent, but it is bad news to those to whom the very idea of repentance is totally repugnant.

5

THE PASTOR AS INSTRUMENT

W hile doing so may introduce confusion, it is impera-
tive that we give "equal time" to the second model,
which is that of the Spirit as the agent and the pastor
primarily as an instrument. It is easy to forget that when
we turn the coin over we are still looking at the same coin,
no matter how different "heads" is from "tails." A coin
without the other side would be defective and non-
negotiable. In order therefore to avoid a premature
commitment to Model One, we need to see that much of
what has been said in promoting it needs to be, while not
contradicted, at least counterpointed.

THE SPIRIT AS INITIATOR

This second model sees the Holy Spirit taking the
initiative, not only in convicting, regenerating, and
sanctifying people, but in supervision of methods as well.
His is not hands-off but hands-on management, at times
in giving a general sense of direction but at other times in
giving minute plans and orders. As Boer points out in
Pentecost and Missions, the early church indicated no

awareness of attempting consciously and systematically to implement the Great Commission.[1] They held no seminars or conferences to devise plans and systems. Witnessing in the power of the Spirit was their system. The Holy Spirit was directly and immediately in charge. Being borne along by His inner fire they preached, prayed, suffered, and rejoiced that they were counted worthy to suffer for Jesus' name. When bogged down in Jerusalem, God dispersed them by means of persecution. But the diffusion was the scattering of Spirit-filled firebrands, who lit fires everywhere they went.

Systematic missionary effort was the initiative of the Spirit, who said to the church at Antioch, "Set apart for me Barnabas and Saul for the work to which I have called them" (Acts 13:2). The immediate response was not to call a committee to devise strategy, but a prayer meeting: "So after they had fasted and prayed, they placed their hands on them and sent them off" (v. 3).

Paul undoubtedly had strong ideas about method. But they were subject to the immediate supervision, and, if necessary, correction of the Holy Spirit. After having "traveled throughout the region of Phrygia and Galatia," it would seem logical to expand to the northwest, into Asia;[2] but to their surprise they "were kept by the Holy Spirit from preaching the word in the province of Asia" (Acts 16:6). Always resilient, Paul and Barnabas concluded that the northeast must be the proper direction, so they proceeded northward. But when "they came to the border of Mysia," and "tried to enter Bithynia," the "Spirit of Jesus would not allow them to" (v. 7). The Spirit had other plans. Thanks to their willingness to bow to the Spirit's plans, the gospel came to Europe—which may explain how we come to be studying church growth.

Furthermore, there is something about the imagery of the Spirit as wind and human methods as sails that leaves one a little uneasy. The image tends to depersonalize the Spirit, and reduce His redemptive activity to the level of mechanical, impersonal law. Do the right thing, and you can be sure of expected results. This is the way electricity operates. But the Spirit? When Jesus used the imagery of the Spirit as wind, He was illustrating the exact opposite of the notion that the Spirit is a neutral force that can be put to work. Rather, "the wind blows wherever it pleases. You hear its sound, but you cannot tell where it comes from or where it is going. So it is with everyone born of the Spirit" (+ 1John 3:8). The Spirit is not like electricity that can be plugged into at will, or trade winds that can be harnessed by clever sailors; but is mysterious and, above all, sovereign. The Spirit is a Person who cannot be corralled or regimented, and whose operations can never quite be fathomed.

This suggests a further weakness in the analogy of wind. The Spirit as trade wind might imply the Spirit's ministry as a generic resource which the church, as a separate entity, can tap at will. This misses a fundamental note of Pentecost. This was not simply a group phenomenon, but primarily individual and personal. The "tongues of fire" did not rest upon the group but "separated and came to rest on each of them." The "all" who were filled with the Spirit was every person, individually, inwardly, privately. While each spoke in a language, the languages varied. There was no religious cloning going on here. This was not an example of mass hypnotism in which individual identity is swallowed up in some kind of corporate personality. This was not a generic coming of the Spirit upon some mythical entity called The Church; it was a coming of the Spirit on persons, one by one.

Therefore in this dispensation there is not a flow of power resting on this mythical entity called The Church, but a coming of the Spirit upon persons, one by one. The ministry of the Spirit may be universal in a sense, yet primarily it is a working through Spirit-filled believers. It isn't a question, then, about the pastor hoisting a sail into the wind; it is a question about the pastor having the wind inside of him. Jesus used the figure of rivers. " 'Whoever believes in me, as the Scripture has said, streams of living water will flow from within him.' By this he meant the Spirit, whom those who believed in him were later to receive" (John 7:38–39).

The book of Acts reveals that the power of the Spirit rests primarily on persons, only secondarily on plans. Therefore a logical inference might be that the first lesson in methodology is for the pastor to understand the necessity of being Spirit-filled. Jack Hyle tells of spending two days and nights in prayer at the grave of his father. "When I left," he said, "I knew I was filled with the Spirit." All methods must grow out of this basic experience and be compatible with it.

We are compelled therefore to take a second look at the model which stresses the Christian worker as agent and the Spirit as dynamic. Perhaps the truth lies closer to the model which sees the Spirit as Agent as well as dynamic, and the Christian worker as Instrument. He plans, but on his knees. He thinks, but in the process seeks guidance. He learns that the Spirit cannot be regimented or compelled by our systems to "deliver the goods." We cannot box Him in by our strategy sessions.

A FLAW IN CHURCH-GROWTH METHODOLOGY?

The tendency to give lip service to the personality of the Spirit and then operate as if He were a law to be manipulated is surprisingly pervasive in much current church-growth methodology. In some cases, kits are offered to anxious pastors, which, if followed, are guaranteed to give specific results. The subtle but unvoiced implication is that the Spirit is compelled to act according to certain spiritual laws that we can use to bring sure-fire success, if we can just discover them. But, of course, this comes dangerously close to sorcery, which as David Hunt makes clear in *The Seduction of Christianity,* is the attempt to manipulate Deity by cultic formulas.

No. The Holy Spirit has been deputized by the Father and the Son as Sovereign of the whole operation, including church growth. He claims sovereignty over strategies and systems as well as spiritual flows of power. Our systems may please Him for a particular church and a particular situation, or they may not. We cannot simply adopt Madison Avenue presuppositions or Madison Avenue know-how and force-fit it into the subjective complexities of a totally different sphere of reality. Rather our immediate methods locally must be sought from the Holy Spirit first, then implemented in His power.

It is true that many systems being promoted include prayer. This in some cases may prove to be the redeeming feature which really does bring the Spirit's blessing on the plans. But it also may simply be in the end a formal activity which becomes a part of the sorcery. Here are four or five components of a watertight plan, and prayer is one of those components. It can be seen as a leverage for gaining certain ends. It is *our* leverage, not the Spirit's instrument for revealing His ends and releasing His power. But if we pray as a method for church growth, we are not necessarily praying in the Spirit; and if not, we are engaging in manipulation. It becomes a leverage rather than the Spirit's mode of intercession.

Rather, let us pray not as a method but as an expression of a broken heart, longing for God's blessing and yearning to intercede for the lost. If we are interceding for the lost with authentic burden we are not doing it in order to achieve church growth. We dare not *use* prayer as an instrument for church growth. Prayer is impudence if it is not worship and if its objective is not the glory of God and the salvation of souls. We may have the glory of God and the salvation of souls without much numerical growth—locally. We may also have numerical growth without glorifying God and without people really being saved. Prayer is a charade if it is only an exercise in the "kit" that is guaranteed to build our church.

On the other hand, it is always proper to pray for greater measures of the Holy Spirit's presence and manifestation. The assumption of Model One was that because the Spirit was given to the church and the world on the Day of Pentecost, fasting and praying for His working was needless; that the winds of the Spirit were always blowing, needing only the erection of our sails. We have seen that while there is truth in this metaphor, by itself it is misleading. Powerful movements of the Spirit are particular to places and times, as, for instance, the Day of Pentecost itself, followed by the "second Pentecost" of Acts 4. The Spirit is active among all people but not universally in the same way or in the same degree. The special manifestations of the Spirit's presence and power we call revivals. Every Christian has an inherent right to experience at least one such revival in his lifetime. When he does, he will never be the same. Therefore, it is always in order to pray for the Holy Spirit to come in unusual power and manifestation. But to attempt to force the Spirit or to whip up a simulation of divine power can only grieve the Spirit and harden hearts.

A PROPER SYNTHESIS

What then? Probably Model One and Model Two need not be mutually exclusive, as long as Model Two is dominant in the pastor's thinking and method.

At Iconium Paul and Barnabas "spoke so effectively that a great number of Jews and Gentiles believed" (Acts 14:1). The effectiveness no doubt was due to the Spirit's anointing upon them, but one gets the impression that there is a reference here also to their skill in speaking. If so, this would be the human side, and consists of an art that can be learned and that will enlarge one's success in soul winning. This Scripture may be said, therefore, to stress the human element.

But the divine element is predominant in Acts 16:13–14 where we read that the "the Lord opened" Lydia's heart "to respond to Paul's message." The human components were in place: (1) They went where she was—"a place of prayer." (2) They got her attention— she was "one of those listening." (3) They faithfully proclaimed the gospel. But the *Lord* opened her heart.

Was this an arbitrary opening, an example of "irresistible grace" and "effectual calling"? No, it was the divine illumination of an already open and hungry heart, for she had gone there to pray, and she was already a "worshiper of God." But now her heart was opened to *these* messengers and to their message of Christ. But she could have resisted. As the Lutherans have sometimes said, "No one can save himself, but he can damn himself." So in our insistence on the sovereign and essential action of the Spirit we stop short of Calvinism.

But we must equally stop short of humanism. At this point we need to return to some things said in the previous chapter. Madison Avenue techniques can capture attention and persuade a percentage to buy. Those same techniques employed by the church can also capture attention and may even persuade troubled people to become religious and join the church. But at some point—perhaps at every point simultaneously—the psychological must be invaded by the spiritual and the purely human influences give way to the Spirit's conviction, or the religiosity and church joining will prove to be temporary and superficial reformations rather than profound transformations. And the attachment will be to people, not to Christ.

The notion, therefore, that Madison Avenue know-how can win people to Christ is weighed in the balance and found wanting. Madison Avenue is not up against human sinfulness plus a web of satanic powers. Madison Avenue's aim is to work with the grain of human nature, not against it. In contrast, the recalcitrance of human nature is the church's supreme obstacle. While, therefore, certain sociological methods of getting attention and dissolving personal antagonisms will help up to a point, beyond that point all methodology must be transposed to a higher and radically different world of reality. The pastor and church that operate on the lower level alone will have nothing on the Day of Judgment but "wood, hay, and stubble" to show for their labors.

Pastors can keep their sanity only by remembering that while their methods affect the number of people they can contact and influence, only the Holy Spirit will turn contacts into conversions; and that because of free will the best of systems will never have universal success. This is true of God's own redemptive plan, which provides for the salvation of all, but assures the salvation only of those who respond.

Therefore, while we will be saddened, we must not despair if in spite of the finest systems of pastors and churches the number who respond and go all the way with God will be relatively small. It is proper for pastors to grieve over those who resist, but not to flagellate themselves for others' resistance. It may be proper to bear guilt for poor plans thoughtlessly put together and nonchalantly carried out, but it is not proper to suppose that if only the plans had been perfect the results would have been total.

It is easy for the ardent soul-winner, who desires to win *everyone* for Christ, to forget Christ's negative pronouncement: "Small is the gate and narrow the road that leads to life, and only a few find it" (Matt. 7:14; cf. Luke 13:23–27). While this should not be used as an excuse for languid effort, it should be a sobering reminder of limited expectations. Sometimes the optimism of church-growth talk almost suggests that if our systems are good enough we can prove Christ wrong.

To hold aloft Model One—the pastor as agent— then shoot it down seems contradictory. But we are faced with real tension, which needs to be acknowledged. The first model seems to fit our theology of free agency, both of the pastor as steward and the unsaved as free agents, while the second model, by which the Holy Spirit's sovereign initiative is stressed, is more congenial to a Calvinistic perception of redemptive dynamics. But perhaps we have seen that excessive reliance on Madison Avenue techniques leads to sociological and humanistic results, while, on the other hand, giving full recognition of the Spirit's indispensable initiative at every level and at every stage does not necessarily lead to a Calvinistic soteriology.

Admittedly there are mysteries in the Spirit's operations which would at times raise questions in one's mind. The Spirit's timing and His degree of power on particular persons and situations might suggest a kind of sovereignty explainable only by Calvinistic premises. But we cannot relinquish our hold on the "whosoever" of John 3:16, and the promise of Jesus that the Spirit would convict the *world* (+1John 16:8). A better explanation lies in our capacity to hinder the Spirit. Unbelief, prayerlessness, indifference, and other forms of sin in the church will grieve the Spirit and choke the channels of blessing.

It is incontestably true that awakening, convicting, regenerating, and sanctifying are ministrations solely of the Spirit and cannot be counterfeited or substituted, and that without these ministrations all religion is spurious and vain. But if the Spirit is going to work in these ways through a local church, three conditions must be met:

1. Our plans, schemes, systems, methods, and polity must be such that the Spirit can and does work through them and is not hindered by them.

2. Even more important is the moral and spiritual state of the church. For the Spirit's primary instrument is the church (including its leadership), but He works through the church on moral terms. The moral and spiritual state of the church will have more to do with the Spirit's redemptive activity than will the particular methods and systems used. The methods may be fine while the spiritual channels may be clogged.

When the Israelites were humiliated by puny little Ai, God said, "Get rid of the sin first. Then I will give you a strategy." And so they did and He did. When the sin was removed and God's strategy employed the victory was won easily.

3. The kingpins in all of this are the pastors. The Spirit must be able to work through them. Their hearts must be pure and their lives unblemished. Perhaps the bottom line after all is expressed by E. M. Bounds, in *Power Through Prayer*: "The church is looking for better methods; God is looking for better men."[3] It is not enough that the Spirit fell on the church at Pentecost. He must come upon God's man or woman today.

6

SOME PARAMETERS OF CHURCH GROWTH

A parameter can be defined as a "relatively fixed and known factor in a complex and fluid situation." Church growth is both complex and fluid. But controlling it are certain limiting factors which are ignored or bypassed at the expense of truth. Every conscientious pastor, who is God's servant rather than the pawn of the secular mood, will try to understand these parameters and allow them to discipline his methodology.

THE PARAMETER OF AUTHENTICITY

We need to pick up on a point made in chapter one. Burgeoning statistics, in themselves, no more prove church growth than excess fat is a proof of health. Swollen membership rolls are not necessarily any more desirable than rising figures on the scales. There is the growth of the balloon and there is the growth of an oak tree. The growth of the balloon is directly proportional to the infusion of hot air. The growth of a tree is a matter of inner vitality. Just so is the authentic growth of a church. Many churches need to begin with qualitative growth before they can safely be trusted with quantitative growth. One district superintendent said after a Sunday in one of his problem churches, "This is a different church. It has been turned around. The atmosphere is holy and loving and beautiful. God is here." Are we sufficiently biblical to perceive that often sound church growth cannot occur without first repairing the foundations? How can there be healthy growth without healthy spiritual life? And how can growth take place in the presence of bickering, jealousy, and carnal divisions?

No amount of church machinery will compensate for the absence of the Spirit's presence in power. So we are reminded that the most important ingredient for doing the Lord's work is to preach the gospel, which has Christ's life in it, with such divine energizing that the Spirit can create the hidden inner processes, and accomplish His ends beyond the noisy turning of church wheels. The Holy Spirit may use our machinery and even work through it, but only if we depend on Him rather than on it.

The implication is that we can build religious organizations called "churches" in the energy of the flesh. They can be quite alive on the humanistic and sociological level. They can be involved in great programs of social work, counseling, fellowship, and fun. There can be something for everyone—drama, athletics, trips, clinics, choirs, and seminars. The program will simulate Christianity. But it can all be without God. The crowds may attend for years without any profound awakenings of soul, without deep upheavals of repentance, without sinners being born again or believers being sanctified wholly.

THE PARAMETER OF INTEGRITY

At the core of every Christianized pastor is integrity. If he does not have integrity, he is self-deceived and a menace in the ministry. Integrity is fidelity to the truth when compromise would be more advantageous. It includes loyalty to one's ordination vows, one's denominational stands, and one's avowed doctrinal commitments. This means for the Wesleyan pastor that holiness is a parameter of church growth. A pastor with integrity will neither promote nor tolerate a growth which is at the expense of doctrinal distinctives.

Holiness is a many-faceted doctrine, involving a positive message of possibilities. There is in it the affirmation of Christ's sanctifying power and His Spirit-infilling offer to the church; His insistence, on pain of forfeiture, that we live holy lives. This doctrine as interpreted by Wesleyans has theological strands that are incompatible with the contemporary interpretation of grace, that separates grace for heaven from grace for life; i.e., the grace which assures us of eternal life is not predicated on a grace that can make us holy now. This bifurcation is hostile to the Wesleyan belief that personal holiness is endemic to personal salvation. Such an anti-holiness bias is deeply rooted in the minds of thousands who have moved into holiness churches within recent years. This is transforming the very nature of these churches, with the result that it is only a matter of time until these professed Wesleyan churches will be essentially Calvinistic.

A possible explanation, at least in part, may be that pastors have been so driven by the pressure for numbers that they have extended their warm welcoming embrace to anyone who seemed to belong to the broad category of evangelical. Many of them are fine people and make good church workers. So they soon are teaching Sunday school classes and elected to official boards. The consequence is church growth, but *not growth with integrity.*

Sometimes this fatal development has occurred not because the pastor intended to let it happen, but because he himself was not doctrinally competent. He was too naïve theologically to recognize basic differences, and too inept as a teacher to know how to inform and shape the thinking of his people. This highlights the hazards of allowing persons to enter the ministry who are not thoroughly trained theologically. Youthful verve, native ability, good intentions, and "terrific" personality do not qualify one to be a pastor.

Or, worse yet, some pastors are simply shallow in their own doctrinal commitments. Their personal creed is soft and pliable. Their secret latitudinarianism means that taking in members whose views on basic theological issues veer to the left or right is no big problem to them. They can be comfortable with variant beliefs in a half dozen different directions. They have no anvil-forged convictions of truth which are non-negotiable. In minor issues of opinion and emphases this "broad-mindedness" may be just good sense, but on the distinctives by which their denomination defines itself, such mushiness is a fatal weakness. Pastors who know the score but refuse to draw clear lines are selling out for bigness. And this is a betrayal of trust.

While faithfulness to our holiness distinctives is not an insurmountable barrier to church growth, the barrier effect is inherently present. It could not be otherwise. The doctrinal distinctives of Adventism, Pentecostalism, Mormonism, and Romanism *of course* constitute roadblocks to growth. They should. What is true of others is equally true of Wesleyans. We can dissipate this obstacle only by blurring our preaching so that everyone is made to feel comfortable with his own beliefs.

Integrity will not permit this. Many pastors, both savvy and courageous, have delineated Wesleyan doctrine with such clarity, and expounded the Scriptures so faithfully, that many have been turned around in their thinking and have become not only sanctified experientially but committed doctrinally. But not so with other hearers. *Because* the pastor is so clear these find it impossible to drift along, enjoying the fellowship and atmosphere, while avoiding the issues of personal need and belief. Sooner or later they are compelled to quit dodging and face up to doctrinal issues. When this happens, unfortunately, some of them quietly slip away.

This we might call negative church growth. Pastors are compelled to face this painful experience as a logical and inevitable outcome of the parameter of integrity. Some of these pastors have seen significant growth in spite of these losses. But they know and observers know that they could have enjoyed much greater growth, if they had been willing to sacrifice integrity.

THE PARAMETER OF PAIN

Some preachers betray a tragic misapprehension of their calling when they suppose that their sole task is to comfort, never disturb; and that they can extend the kingdom of God without birth throes. Their idea of church life seems to be a non-stop religious celebration, everything light and airy, reassuring, free and lively, with only affirmation, optimism, and positive thinking. In their philosophy, a service is successful only in so far as it makes everyone happy. To make people uncomfortable is the supreme pastoral no-no.

A recent article in a secular magazine describing such

a popular superchurch portrayed the approach by the title, "Feel-Good Theology." It was the sharp appraisal of a secular mind. Even the world senses that something is awry if feeling good is the supreme objective of a total church program.

But the pastor of such a church needs to stop long enough to ask himself what Christianity is all about. It is a religion of radical redemption, making radical promises but imposing radical demands. The assumptions of Christianity are that people are lost in sin and on their way to a devil's hell; that Christ died to save us from this horrible plight and worse destiny; that salvation is only through Christ; that it is available on thoroughly moral terms, involving faith, yes, but a faith born of repentance—a repentance which may require restitution (even today!). Furthermore, the terms include walking in that light which leads to total consecration, death to the rebellious ego, and ongoing obedience.

Now there is pain in all of this. A pastor who supposes that his job is simply to boost and jollify simply doesn't know what he is about. If he is to be God's shepherd and God's voice he cannot spare his people the anguish of self-discovery. Faithfulness will result in the throb of guilt and lead to the profound suffering of true repentance. Nor can he spare believers the painful process of crucifixion. Rather, his preaching must be one of the Spirit's instruments in driving the nails. If his ministry smooths over the realities of his hearers' condition and exudes a false comfort, he is in the sight of God guilty of high crimes. He is a false prophet who says, "Peace, peace," when there is no peace (Jer. 6:14).

As important as it is to comfort the disturbed, it is equally important to disturb the comfortable. A lady in Australia began attending a nearby holiness church, but soon discontinued. When sought out by lay visitors, she explained, "The preaching makes me feel like a sinner." Later when she was soundly converted in the Billy Graham campaign, she not only resumed attending but in due time became a member and remained loyal until her death. Perhaps the preaching that made her "feel like a sinner," though at first rejected, was what prepared her for the Billy Graham campaign some months later. At least when filling out the card and naming the pastor whom she desired to call on her, she specified him who had made her feel like a sinner! Down beneath the initial rejection in many persons there is an intuitive awareness of truth in the pulpit.

Much is made these days of the duty of the church to comfort. The peril is that the church sometimes tries to comfort without sufficient discrimination. For the unsaved person, the kind of comfort needed is the planting of hope that there is a way out for him. But too often comfort is interpreted as affirming the sinner as he is and making him feel good about himself. This is premature comfort, and is out of place.

Before comfort comes conviction. This is the Bible order. People must feel bad about themselves before they will come to Jesus; and only when they come to Jesus do they have any biblical ground for feeling good about themselves. So let the church beware of aborting the process.

A church and its pastor are successful not just if they are good comforters, but if God is able to use them to convict as well as comfort. This means preaching the "whole will of God" (Acts 20:27)—the negatives as well as the positives, red lights as well as green, the law as well as the gospel, God's wrath as well as God's love. And the necessity of purity as well as the offer of pardon.

In a review of *The Subversion of Christianity* by Jacques Ellul (Eerdmans), Daniel B. Clendenin says that evangelicals can profit from Ellul's "reminder that without the 'theology of the cross' any 'theology of glory' is a perversion"[1] He adds, "In Luther's words . . . 'faith is a perturbing thing,' and it brings with it the certainty of suffering, offense and scandal, not worldly security, prestige and success."

Surely, if anyone should understand this, it should be the holiness preacher. The point is that a holiness church and a holiness pastor dare not operate on a risk-free platform. They must determine to place integrity, courage, and faithfulness at the very center of their methodology. Only this is true love, either for God or man.

THE PARAMETER OF THE
GREAT PARADOX

One of the paradoxes of the Christian religion is the sense of urgency that should rightfully be on us versus the unhurried calmness and deliberateness of Jesus. We tend to panic as we study world statistics and see how the population is outstripping evangelism. In response we contrive great schemes for stepping up the pace, exponentially if possible, of our outreach. At the local level we feel the pressure of reaching the lost *now*. When we reach them, we hothouse disciple them in order to accelerate the process and reach more and more faster and faster. In our hurry we have a hard time with Jesus' calmness.

But most of all do we find it difficult to reconcile our sense of urgency with Jesus' metaphors and parables. He says we change our world as salt and light. He didn't seem to be so concerned about the quantity of salt as He was about the quality of its saltiness. And He warned us not to put our light under a bushel basket, but on a stand where it can illuminate its surrounding space. Its sole mission is illumination, and it accomplishes its mission simply by shining.

And so many parables point to the undramatic, maddeningly slow processes of growth. The parables of the sower, the tares, the mustard seed, yeast—all quietly preach the certainty of results but the futility of haste. Jesus reminded the disciples that the energy of the farmer does not put life in the seed, and cannot alter or speed up the tedious process of production, "first the stalk, then the head, then the full kernel in the head" (Mark 4:28).

All of which is to say that our hurry and bustle to win the world and make presto saints is fine and noble but destined for exasperating frustration. For in the kingdom of God the two truths of the paradox are with us always. The Commission is there, commanding, imperious, urgent. But the process is there, too, which refuses to be pushed. As Stacy and Paula Rinehart remind us, "People cannot be hustled into the Kingdom of God."[2] Spiritual awakening has its *kairos* moments, but mostly its slow hidden influences. New converts can be nurtured, shepherded, and guarded (and must be). But spiritual progress with many of them will refuse to sync with our discipling schedules.

It takes years to grow a saint, even a sanctified one. And while crowds may be drawn in it takes years to build a spiritual church. So we are caught in the tension of the Great Paradox. The outreach pressure and the inward process struggle along side by side, even pulling against each other, the one demanding haste, the other calling for time and patience. Perhaps this is one reason God has given to the church different types of ministries: apostles (missionaries?), prophets, evangelists, and pastors and teachers (Eph. 4:11).

We should not allow the Great Paradox to cut the nerve of our passion. It might, however, be a healthful corrective to shift the focus of our passion just a bit from church growth, per se, to the conversion of sinners, the sanctification of believers, and their upbuilding in the most holy faith. Then we will be less apt to make church growth an end in itself, achieved in appearance but at the expense of its predicates.

But we must return to a reaffirmation of our strength. Holiness is what every church needs, what faithful pastors long for in their people, and what will make for rock-ribbed stability in the long run[3]. It does not have to be presented negatively or unrealistically, with the result that people are worn out trying to be holy. When this is the case, the presentation has been wrong.

And holiness faithfulness does not mean that we have to be small. We should go after the crowds, but not by means of cheap bait. Most holiness churches could and should be twice as large as they are. There is no virtue in smallness for smallness' sake. As for superchurches, let us build them if we can. But it takes a superman to build a superchurch without compromise. It takes a man who has looked the dangers—and the parameters—squarely in the face, and has committed himself before God not to soft-pedal his message or methods for the sake of numbers. In the long run God will honor fidelity. A faithful holiness ministry will still be pushing back the darkness and impacting a broken world long after the froth and foam spectaculars have been forgotten.

Part Two
OUTREACH DIMENSIONS

7

REACHING PEOPLE—WAYS THAT WORK

A t every point one's goals must be clear: "Reaching people" means winning them to Christ and getting them into the church. After reaching them comes nurturing, leading them to full salvation, putting them to work, and helping them all the way to heaven. But first we must reach them.

While conversion and church membership are the consummation points of reaching people, many preparatory steps and stages mark the way. In this the pastor is the leader, but the whole church is involved. People who are to be reached must come not just to the preacher but to the church. Therefore the pastor-church team together must operate in such a way that they will create a web of influences extending throughout an entire community. These influences usually proceed along some ordinary and natural lines. Assuming that prayer impregnates all other activities, the Spirit customarily works through the psychological and sociological dynamics of human nature, both as created and as fallen.

PUBLIC AWARENESS

People must become aware that this church exists. This may be brought about by advertising as one possibility. Regular newspaper advertising, radio or TV spots, various mailings, will keep the church in the public eye. Even telemarketing has a place—about which more will be said later.

An alert pastor can cultivate good relations with the religion editor of the local newspaper through whom judiciously written and timely news stories can occasionally find their way into the paper.

People will become aware of the church through neat, well-located signs. They will also be attracted to the church by beautifully kept lawns and buildings. A prominent location will multiply this awareness.

To a limited extent a community-wide awareness and stock of goodwill accrue through the recitals, cantatas, pageants, concerts, and films (missionary or evangelistic) that constitute a part of a church's ministry to its own people. However, if a pastor relies on these events as his primary mode of outreach, he may be springing a booby trap on himself. It is an easy way to get people in, which in the long run may prove to be a cheapie way. For in time people will come to see this church as a glorified religious Chatauqua—a wholesome, pleasant, upbeat entertainment center. The spiritual power will be diluted (if present at all) and people sedated into religious blahs. The more Sunday services are diverted from preaching the Word the more the people's appetites will be perverted, and the less interest they will have in the Word. To resort weakly to this easy method of operating a church is already a confession of failure. While occasional special attractions may foster awareness and lead to valuable contacts, an excessive dependency on this mode of church growth will produce a house of cards not a New Testament *ecclesia.*

The best awareness is that which comes by word of mouth: neighbors, fellow-workers, other patients in hospitals. "Yes, I've heard of that church," is the first signal of awareness; and thousands of people in the area should be able to say that, *and say it with a smile.*

PASTORAL PUBLIC RELATIONS

If pastors are pushy, demanding, and crotchety in their dealings with newspaper editors and other media persons, or if they or their associates do not know how to write, they will create antagonism and close this door. But let the pastor think of these people as human beings who need him more than he needs them. He should cultivate warm, friendly relations with them not as a means of *using* them but as a means of serving them, his church, and the community.

One pastor, whose church benefited by far more newspaper space than was their share, was asked his secret. He said, "When I came to town, I immediately introduced myself to various editors. I got to know them on a first-name basis. There is not a week that I have not had some association with them—playing golf, having coffee, or even sending flowers to their wives."

That may be going too far in "kissing the Blarney stone," but the principle is sound: cultivate these persons. These are days when in some quarters the hostility between media and church is barely checked beneath a thin veneer of civility. While the pastor must be willing to take moral stands openly, and must never stoop to fawning over media people (which will prompt them to despise him in their hearts), he does not need to allow an adversarial relationship to develop by his own bungling.

After all, they hold the trump card of publicity. If they get it in for a pastor, they can ruin him.

If a pastor cannot work with all the heads of newspapers, radio, and TV in his city, let him find two or three persons of clout with whom he can safely be intimate. They will guide him—without attempting to compromise him—and at times run interference. There are Christian media people. Pastors should know them, lean on them, and listen to them—certainly never take advantage of them or embarrass them. When a journalist or radio person burns his fingers a time or two coming to the aid of clergy who prove unworthy, even the best of them become wary and frosty.

Business people—including media professionals— are supersensitive to trickiness in the clergy. Their own practices may be far from lily white, but they idealize men of the cloth. This is one reason they hound a case of dereliction to death. Their rage and cynicism is the backhand of disappointment. They would like to think that there is at least one profession that is honest and genuine all the way through. When they are let down by the clergy, they are more bitter than they would be with the same hanky-panky in doctors or lawyers.

Furthermore, it is the fine points of ethics that these observers are sensitive about. IRS agents can testify to the sloppy thinking and shady practices uncovered among clergy—many of whom profess to be honest; but their kind of honesty does not meet the fine points of the law. Bankers, also, could tell some tales. The issues that trouble them are not blank lies, just verbal padding. Not robbing the bank, but misleading it. One banker became interested in a church and began attending. In fact, he became a close confidant and advisor to the pastor. For two years they worked closely on a number of projects. But gradually the banker withdrew and dissociated himself completely from that church. He confided to a friend that he became disillusioned by the ease with which the pastor could resort to strategies in dealing with his people, which kept some facts and objectives under the table. Yet the young pastor was a devout man, who would not have viewed his own methods as being manipulative or questionable. The world often thinks more logically about these matters than we do. The banker knew that all sorts of trickery go on daily in the business world, but he did not expect to find a Christian pastor operating on that level.

If, therefore, a pastor would succeed in a community, let him cultivate amiable public relations; but above all, so conduct himself that he will earn among people of the world a good name. A "good name" is still "more desirable than great riches" (Prov. 22:1)—or high salaries or fine parsonages.

CONTACT RECEPTIVITY

Face-to-face contacts between pastor and unchurched folk are of two kinds: planned and unplanned, purposeful and casual.

1. *Casual contacts* should be taking place every day and can occur anywhere. Some pastors are more gifted than others with an outgoing personality. It is easy for them to pass the time of day and chat a bit. Their warmth is so natural that it is irresistible. People feel at ease and respond in kind. Every such contact breaks down barriers, dissipates fears and prejudices, and conditions persons toward future more purposeful contacts.

In a way this ability to create rapport almost instantly is one of a pastor's greatest assets. It opens doors into hearts and homes. Pastors who by nature are reserved and shy must cultivate the art of bonhomie. For hundreds of casual but pleasant contacts mean hundreds of friends, and generate receptivity everywhere. Later when these persons are in the hospital, or called on purposefully, the receptivity is already there.

A pastor thus spreads his or her influence through a whole community by casual contacts. They may take place in barber shops, elevators, stores, on the street, anywhere. So important is this that the pastor who really wants to reach people had better be out among them every day, in all kinds of settings.

And let him be properly attired and mind his manners. But behind the manners must be human kindness which radiates in unmistakable genuineness. People were drawn to Jesus—children, women, sinners. Yes, men too. Why shouldn't they be drawn to a pastor—not primarily as a pastor, at first, but as a man or a woman.

2. *Purposeful contacts* especially depend on receptivity for their success. If a person is open toward a pastor and is glad to see him, half the battle is won. Every such purposeful contact can deepen confidence, nourish friendship, and nudge him just a little closer to a decision for Christ.

A purposeful contact is a conversation that a pastor has *in his role as a minister* and with a religious objective in mind. It may take place in a hospital room, an office, the pastor's study, a home. It may be instigated in a variety of ways—a call from the person himself, or from a friend or relative, a church member who knows the need, or from something read in the newspaper.[1]

Even though the pastor may have met these persons and established a bond of friendliness, their receptivity *now,* in this more formal situation, is uncertain. Therefore, while the pastor should be straightforward, he should be cautious and tactful.

A STRUCTURAL APPROACH TO IDENTIFYING PROSPECTS

An alert pastor will not lack for prospects. They will multiply like rabbits, if he simply follows *flow lines* and *access points*.

1. A *flow line* is the natural current of interest fanning out through relatives, fellow-workers, and neighbors. Very few are without this flow of influence toward someone—wife, husband, cousins, employees, out through the human relationships that bind people together. They are conductors of spiritual power in many different directions. Let the pastor follow this flow. One person is converted. He is the line to his family and to his social circle. All of these persons in the flow line hear about the change in him. They are shocked, pleased, skeptical, scornful, or wistful. But they are curious. Follow the flow line to these people.

2. An *access point* or *handle* is an event or structure which opens doors. The Sunday school roll is a gold mine of access points. Every child on the roll is an entree into that child's home. Absentees provide opportunities to show the kind of love and interest that families find irresistible. A hospital call is an access point, either to other patients or the patient's family. And what a plethora of access points are afforded by funerals and weddings. Every such event extends a pastor's influence. His name and face become known to more people, friendly responsive feelings are generated, and contact opportunities multiply exponentially, probably far beyond the pastor's ability to pursue. Any pastor worth his salt who really wants to reach people will soon be loaded with notes and names.

REACHING YOUNG PARENTS

I have mentioned the Sunday school roll as a source of *access points*. This should include the home department and the cradle roll. Especially is the cradle roll a method "made in heaven." Young parents are perhaps more receptive than any other group. They are profoundly moved and sobered as they look into the helpless, innocent face of their firstborn. A new surge of responsibility grips them. No matter how far from God their present lifestyle may be, they instinctively feel a burst of desire to be good parents. If at this time an alert cradle roll supervisor asks to enroll the baby, rare is the mother who (if not already actively church connected) will not leap at the opportunity, usually with the approval of the young father.

Suddenly, and so simply, a church connection has been established. If the cradle roll supervisor is on the job, she will be in that home monthly (at least), inquiring, admiring, extending help, and leaving the provided literature. Likely, the young mother will begin thinking of this as her church, even though she may never have set foot in the door. Sooner or later she will—when Cradle Roll Day comes, for sure; and her husband will follow. Sooner or later, also, occasions will arise for the pastor to be drawn into this little circle. If no one blows it, the probable outcome will be a family reached for Christ and the church.

In three of this writer's pastorates, the cradle roll, conducted by his wife (the most logical person always, if possible), constituted a substantial section of the overall ministry, and accounted for an impressive percentage of the statistical gains. But my wife knew how to do it. She was a friend to the mothers, and faithful to them in their typical young-mother problems. The literature was not only distributed, but explained. For the first birthday of each child she made a small cake, topped it with a tiny candle, and delivered it to the home, with suitable fanfare. Often this would be the occasion for the pastor—her husband—to put in his appearance. So if the pastor had not become involved before, he was now. The upshot was that in many cases it was only a matter of time until not only was the child's name on the cradle roll but the parents' names were on the church roll.

THE DOOR OF TROUBLE

The most poignant kind of access point is trouble. While being a caring people and a caring pastor does not define the extent of our mission as holiness churches, it is part of that mission. Trouble is often the first point of solid contact. When people are overwhelmed, beyond their ability to cope, they will welcome an extended hand, whether the hand belongs to a Mormon, Catholic, or Wesleyan. They are heartsick, bewildered, trapped. The problem may be domestic, physical, legal, financial. Maybe they have never given the church a thought. But now they are glad for the preacher to involve himself, for in him (and in his people) they see hope.

This may not yet be conviction of sin. It is not necessarily repentance. It is stark need. A man out of work with hungry mouths to feed, a mother who has no way to get to the hospital to see her sick child, a battered wife, the parents of a runaway, or a pregnant teenager do not need sermons, yet. They need love and understanding on a practical nuts-and-bolts level. If these persons are handled correctly, conviction, conversion, and assimilation may unfold down the line. Their spiritual welfare will of course always be the uppermost concern of a true man or woman of God.

Helping people in trouble is often a test of a pastor's motives. Let him pray that God will so wash his eyes with tears of real compassion that he will not see (1) this merely as a golden opportunity to reach those elusive conference goals; or (2) conversely, be tempted to ignore the need because "these are not the sort we want in our church." While it is proper to think normally of "reaching people" in terms of both conversion and church membership, let us not be coldly calculating and self-serving in our proffered or withheld benevolence. We may reach some people for heaven by helping them in their hour of deep need without ever getting them into our church.

8

DRAWING THE NET

J esus said to Simon and Andrew, "I will make you fishers of men" (Matt. 4:19). Naturally they would think of fishing in terms of the method with which they were most familiar: using nets. The process would be to spread the net in the water in such a way that the fish would swim into it, then at the proper time drawing it in. Spreading the net is what we have been talking about. Through a complex network of small events people have become encircled by this church's influence. They rightfully belong to its sphere of outreach. They are part of its "constituency." By this time they are more or less friendly. They are more or less aware of their spiritual need. They may be attending occasionally or even regularly. No doubt their names are on a list somewhere: pastor's prospect list, Sunday school roll, home department, youth department, cradle roll. Perhaps they play on a church team.

THE PURPOSEFUL CONTACT

All this is good, but not good enough. The church is after them for Christ. The church seeks their salvation.

Nothing less. It is proper therefore to attend now to the question of drawing the net. Peter and Andrew knew that a fisherman who put his net out and never drew it in was either a fool or playing games. It is not putting out nets that lands fish, but pulling in nets.

Therefore, the pastor and church that would reach people must know when and how to draw the net. The objective is the crisis of sound conversion, when people actually experience the new birth.

The pastor and his people operate in the confidence that, unless fatally resisted, the web of influences which Providence has thrown around these prospects over the months or years will bring them to a readiness for decision. Happy are these people when the circle of significant persons around them have the skill and wisdom to know how to capitalize on this readiness, and bring them to Jesus.

There is no ironclad rule governing this process, excepting one: sensitivity to the Holy Spirit. Since we cannot regiment the Holy Spirit, we must learn to let Him prompt us. Times, settings, and methods are almost as diverse as the persons to be won. People may be led to Jesus in a hospital, an office (less likely), their homes, the pastor's study, or at a public altar.

There is still a place for the traditional revival campaign (see chapter ten). Many who are today solidly in the church can testify that at a certain stage in their spiritual awakening someone persuaded them to attend such a revival meeting, where under clear gospel preaching their hunger crystallized and they found the Lord. The church that abandons this kind of effort loses a powerful weapon in its armory; or to return to the figure of the net, a kind of net which by no means is outmoded. The revival gathers the energies of the entire church into this concentrated endeavor, and provides incentives for lay action in the form of invitations and hospitality, which are not present in the same degree in the usual run of events. Furthermore, the high tide of prayerfulness, public interest, and emotional excitement that mark a well-conducted revival contribute to bringing to white heat the conviction of the unconverted.

As tempting as it is however to discuss revival methods, at this point we need to focus on the pastor in his own net management. We have previously mentioned the pastor's "purposeful contacts." No matter what the occasion or how brief this purposeful contact may be, there should be some effort to move the person Godward and churchward. This much is always in order for a minister of the gospel. Some religious word will normally be *expected*. People know what a minister is supposed to be about! The setting, the need, and the degree of receptivity will aid the wise pastor in knowing whether this first contact should extend to a word of prayer, perhaps also a word of Scripture. When the receptivity is present people are more apt to be pleased than offended if the pastor closes the visit by saying, "Do you mind if I offer a word of prayer?" They are apt to be disappointed if he does not.

Occasionally the pastor may discover that the receptivity is not so ripe as he thought. Some degree of hostility or rejection may surface. In such cases let the pastor back off and seek to cover the situation with that degree of graciousness and understanding which may lead to greater receptivity later on. He should be careful not to spoil his future chances by insistence or pushiness.

Let the pastor remember that the Holy Spirit is always working. He is preparing people for the pastor's ministrations. But they may not be ready yet. Give the Holy Spirit time, keep praying, and the person or persons may be ready the next time a contact is made. Of course an initial rebuff should not discourage the preacher from a second or third or fourth try.

GROWING CONFIDENCE

An initial contact which is positive—even if not immediately fruitful—will lead to subsequent contacts, by the pastor and (one hopes) by others. The result will be developing ease, personal affinity, growing interest, and soon the beginning of involvement.

This involvement may at first be primarily on a social level. One church developed a Thursday night informal social time in private homes to which friends at work or neighbors could be invited. It was a relatively homogeneous grid, consisting of young couples who worked at the same mill. About a dozen or so couples began to show up, children and all. Most of them were gun-shy but curious, and beneath the surface, hungry. Fortunately the events were sparked by a young female dynamo who could joke, banter, play games, and feed, or lead choruses, testify, and pray, all equally well; and she always managed to get all seven in before the evening was out. She created an atmosphere in which the unchurched folk did not feel threatened, and they were fascinated by the naturalness and sincerity with which she eased into the devotional end of the evening.[1]

Needless to say before long these young families were attending Sunday school. For a while they would slip out after Sunday school and go home, but gradually they got over their fear of church. In due course the pastor was able to lead most of these couples to the Lord and into church membership. Many of them became the backbone of that church.

What was happening? On the hidden level, the Holy Spirit was prodding, convicting, creating hunger. But on the human level *confidence* was building. That is an indispensable process. It is an unfolding flower. Most people's first tentative response is on the social and friendship level. Happy is the pastor who isn't carrying the whole weight of reaching people on his own shoulders, but who has lively committed lay people who are willing to be social nets for Jesus.

But at first people are skittish because they are often full of misconceptions and fears. Whether watching at a safe distance or attending regularly they are observing keenly. They want to be sure that what they are seeing— the friendliness, helpfulness, personal caring—is for real.

It is only when confidence has been thoroughly established and people feel comfortable around the pastor and church activities that they really let their guard down and become receptive to personal evangelism. By this time their hunger has reached a peak of intensity. They are ready to acknowledge their sins in honesty and humility because they find themselves surrounded by believable love. Concerned Christians have taken them into their circle, and in this new atmosphere it becomes easier to weep, to confess, to confide, to pray like a child. These things done with strangers are apt to be theatrics.

Some pastors are adept in leading people to a decision in the first real private contact. It cannot be denied that occasionally we discover a person who is truly ready, like fruit just waiting to be plucked. The necessary confidence seems to rise intuitively.

But about such conversions two things need to be said. First, in the cases most apt to be genuine and lasting, there is a background, sometimes a lengthy one, which has already conditioned the person to be receptive to a gospel presentation. They probably have been around church all their lives, or at least have powerful memories of the years when they were. Such persons are not hostile to preachers. Very likely at some time in the past they have already had a religious experience. They know what this is all about and what they ought to do. They are relieved to have someone finally bring them face to face with the issue of their spiritual need.

The second thing is less reassuring. Too many of these out-of-the-blue conversions prove superficial. These persons are the wayside soil in our Lord's parable. In many cases the psychology at work is very simple: it is the impact of a stronger personality over a weaker. Many people are awed, almost hypnotized, in the presence of a minister, just as they are in the presence of the doctor. The skillful clergyman can lead a half-scared, intimidated person through the Four Spiritual Laws (or some other approach), with very little depth of involvement, either of resistance or comprehension. But people easily won may be easily lost (cf. Matt. 13:2–21). And if afterward they come to feel that they have "been had," the reaction can postpone real regeneration many years; or create such a hostile hang-up that repentance may be forever forestalled.

What applies to one-on-one contacts applies equally to mass evangelism. Too much pressure, which is more personality than Holy Spirit, can wreak untold damage. In one revival meeting parents of an unsaved young man prayed and worked to get him into a service and finally succeeded one night. The preacher had a high-pressure message and issued a high-pressure altar call. And extended. And extended. The glamorous lady evangelist left the pulpit, put her pretty face close to his, and inveigled him into going to the altar and making a profession. But the next morning when he awoke, as from a binge, he felt he had been made a fool of and refused thereafter to step foot in that or any other church. He had been swept off his feet by a powerful personality, and the evangelist completely short-circuited whatever work the Holy Spirit was trying to do.

SKILLFUL MIDWIFERY

In bringing spiritual babes to birth it is important that those who help them understand at least the rudiments of the theology of salvation. While there may be a lot of trouble that prompts people to come to Jesus as "The Answer" to their problems, this will lead merely to a psychological religious experience and false hopes, if deeper down there is not a sense of sin and a longing for salvation from *it*. Really, Jesus has never promised health, wealth, and prosperity, or that He would be a universal panoply against trouble. He came as a Savior from sin. Unless this is what seekers really want, they will profess a relationship with Him, which is inherently defective because self-deceptive. And they will see Jesus as a means to a "new high" or to a social advantage or as a talisman against bad luck.

Furthermore, it is dangerously delusive to try to elicit a profession of faith by verbal instruction alone. It is easy to get a person to acquiesce about his sinfulness in the abstract, to agree verbally about God's love and the purpose of the Cross, then verbally to "accept" Christ. At some point this sinner-needing-to-be-saved must pray. *Really* pray. It must be an I-Thou meeting. The Holy Spirit needs an opportunity to seal this personal meeting with Christ by His divine sense of acceptance. The joy and peace must not be the product of a syllogism but a divine implanting. Only God knows when the heart is truly penitent, and only God can forgive and create within the wonderful sense of forgiveness. At this point the Rubicon to reach people is crossed. They are now in the kingdom and, in the spiritual sense, already in the church.

The battle for full holiness, maturity, and usefulness is yet to come.

These chapters on reaching people may be summarized this way: If a pastor and his church want to reach people they must go after them. There are no shortcuts. Mass evangelism must never be despised or abandoned (see chapter ten). But neither public evangelism nor special attractions will substitute for the person-to-person ministry. If a strong church is to be built, the pastor and his associates—both lay and staff—need to handle every stone.

9

SYSTEMS OF ACCELERATION

T here are times when some heroic system for accelerating the pace of reaching people can be profitably used.

THE COMMUNITY SURVEY

The more traditional method has been the house-to-house survey, by which an entire community is inventoried in a short time. This involves a large number of trained volunteers who are able to ask the right questions and record the right information. Many different approaches have been used. For a few years the most common was the lead question, "Do you know of any children in this neighborhood who are not in Sunday school?" Other pastors preferred to take the bull by the horns and say up front, "We are from the _____ Church and we are looking for people who do not attend Sunday school and who might be interested in ours." Or: "We are from the _____ Church on the corner of Second and Main Streets, and we are making a survey. Would you mind telling us if you have a church

connection? . . .Which church is it? . . .Are you attending? . . .Do you know anything about our church? Have
you ever attended?"

Questions vary in nature and must be instantly
flexible, for the aim is for the questioning to develop into
a friendly chat. Always some item of advertising should
be left, if the person will take it.

The ultimate value of the survey method depends on
the pastoral follow-up. If people show some interest, even
mild, and confess to being inactive, this data will be of
little value if these persons never hear from the church or
its pastor again. It is better for a survey not to be made
than made and not pursued.

Often such surveys are conducted interdenomina-
tionally. At times, if such projects are launched by the
local ministerial association, the holiness churches should
cooperate. However, they will provide, in all likelihood,
the lion's share of workers and get the mouse's share of
benefits. The reason for this is that the survey card will list
the person's church preference, and all the cards of a
particular denomination or church must be given to that
pastor, with a "gentleman's agreement" that these persons
are now off-limits to the other pastors. Since the vast
majority of persons surveyed will name a mainline
denomination (which they may not have attended for
twenty years), it is obvious that the survey can result in a
straightjacket for evangelical, and especially Wesleyan,
pastors. For this reason some holiness pastors prefer to
collect their own data.

Many people have been reached for Christ and the
church by means of such surveys. In the majority of
typical communities they are still promising; in many
urban areas, such as high rise apartment complexes, they
are virtually impossible. The high percentage of working

women, also, militates against this method—though that can be more of an alibi than a solid negative argument.

BUS MINISTRY

By putting into place a bus ministry, many churches have enjoyed a period of rapid growth, at least in Sunday school attendance, resulting ultimately in increased church membership. Others have attempted it but experienced more problems than blessing. In general there is not so much enthusiasm about bus ministries as there was a few years ago. Churches have learned the hard way that a successful bus ministry is costly in money and energy, and that it has in it potential headaches.

The chief requisites are (1) a fleet of buses and (2) a large group of unselfish, dependable, highly organized and highly motivated workers—whose motivation lasts beyond the newness. The buses are costly not only to buy but to maintain. The possibilities are great if the church is fortunate enough to have a large number of mechanically inclined working men who can service the buses, keep them presentable in appearance, washed and cleaned regularly; and an additional number of licensed, willing, cheerful, year-round drivers plus a corps of bus mothers or dads plus (again) bus pastors who can scout out children, and mothers and grandfolk who will ride the bus and then follow up on the riders week after week if necessary. Oh—and one or two items more: facilities to handle a sudden influx of rowdy children, together with an enlarged, trained, and ultra-patient teaching staff. (For many of these children will be undisciplined and untamed little hooligans, who will have no idea of proper decorum in church.)

But if all this can be put in place, the rewards in the long run will be rich, not just in statistical gains but in boys and girls who will be saved and grow up in the church to become some day the bus drivers and the teachers. Some of them will go off to holiness colleges and become preachers and/or missionaries. Many others will marry in the church and found strong Christian homes.

However, this is such a multifaceted ministry and so demanding that no pastor should attempt it unless he has committed laypeople to help carry the load.

TELEMARKETING

The new method which has in some areas taken the church by storm is *telemarketing*. This is highly offensive to some people, but perhaps no more so than having to respond to a knock at the door. In either case there is a certain invasion of privacy which today's citizen has become increasingly touchy about. It has yet to be seen whether telemarketing, in particular, will in the long run create more negative hostility toward the church using it than the benefits will justify.[1]

Yet a certain percentage of people are lonely or in need, and will eagerly respond to a loving voice. Radio and TV ministries, which for years have operated banks of telephone counselors and received probably millions of calls, have sufficiently demonstrated that the telephone is the communication medium of choice for many people. Of course the difference here is that they take the initiative and make the call, whereas in telemarketing the church initiates the call. The very people who, being in the right mood, may phone an anonymous counselor a thousand miles away may be irritated when a local religious group calls and wakens them out of a sound nap. Obviously, therefore, variables exist which those who would under-take this method need to think about carefully. Perhaps telemarketing is most promising (1) in the case of a small church struggling for identity in a new and growing community, and (2) as a church-planting technique.

A superintendent reported to me that one of his smaller churches had ten families who were faithful but could not seem to break out of the 50–60 attendance bracket. Prayerfully, and after much study of methods and training of volunteers, they launched an intensive telemarketing effort. They made 20,000 calls, netting 1650 people who showed enough interest to allow their names to be put on a mailing list. Items of mail were sent each week for four weeks, culminating in a highly publicized Visitor Sunday, when 252 people attended. In subsequent weeks the attendance leveled off to 160–180—still a 300% increase. The pastor brought as many as would respond into an intensive two months of discipling, then received 57 of them into church membership on profession of faith. One requirement imposed was that they be willing to function in a small group under a leader to whom they promised to be amenable.

This report illustrates what must be done if a telemarketing effort is not going to inundate a church with a hundred different doctrines, notions, motives, goals, temperaments, backgrounds, and emotional biases that refuse to be melded into a body conformable to the denomination. Out of a crowd of respondents such as this some would want instant access to power and seek to try to create a church in their own image. Others would propagandize former doctrinal positions, and subvert the doctrinal position of the church. The moral is that only a wise, courageous pastor, who knows how to handle people and who keeps a firm hand on the wheel, had better attempt telemarketing.

Three classes of people are most likely to respond to telemarketing. The first—which is the group most highly desired—are people who are just plain hungry-hearted.

They have been secretly longing for some opportunity to connect with a church because they have come to see their need of God and all the church stands for.

The second class consists of people who are disgruntled with where they are now worshiping or with past church experiences, and are eager to try something new. Some of these persons have valid complaints and in a proper setting will make great church members. But others are simply church tramps, and will soon drift off; or, if they stay, may prove to be troublemakers. I heard J. B. Chapman say at a pastor's retreat, "There are two steps in establishing a new church. One is to gather a few charter members. The next step is to get rid of the charter members." Of course he was talking tongue-in-cheek, for he would have been the last to slur the many honorable and saintly charter members who have held the work together through rough days. But perhaps there was just enough truth in his quip to justify it.

The third class consists of people whose background matches the denomination of the calling church, but who have lost touch for various reasons and are excited about the prospect of their own kind of church becoming available in this neighborhood or town.

The great temptation of the pastor or church planter who would utilize telemarketing is to hide the real purpose and the real identity of the church. This is always the mark of a false cult. Furthermore, it savors of the deceptive sales tactic of "bait and switch," which in the business world is illegal. Not that the caller needs to plunge into a theological lecture the first contact, but neither should any basic mark of the church be camouflaged. Naturally the first appeal will be at the point of the widest common denominator—the Bible, Christ, salvation. It is essential and only fair that some way be designed to let an interested person understand that the church is Protestant and traditionally orthodox. They need to know that they are not being approached by one of the many modern cults.

If there is too much fuzziness and the appeal is simply to meet for a religious good time, the temptation will be strong to keep the platform nebulous in order to keep people coming. But a blurred platform will result either in losing them when they discover what this church *really* stands for, or else the blur will become permanent, and the church remain a nondescript community fellowship with a broad, indiscriminate appeal. Down the road when some unwary pastor tries to move the group toward a more focused doctrinal and denominational commitment he will be fought tooth and nail, and probably lose his scalp.

While it is premature to rule out the possibility of new churches starting full grown with 200 or more members through telemarketing and becoming viable holiness churches, the difficulties of molding such a group in such a direction are formidable. The task will require a much higher level of pulpit competence and a much more powerful spirit of continuous revival than is characteristic of the typical established church.

Without denial, any effort which results in one person being saved and reaching heaven is worthy of our respect. But whether or not telemarketing is the best evangelizing and church-growing method available in most communities remains an open question. The jury is still out. When the dust has settled the probabilities are that the quiet, gradual infiltration of a community described in chapters seven and eight will prove the method of church growing most durable in the long run.

10

THE REVIVAL CAMPAIGN

T his is the third form of heroic measure for acceleration of the church-growth process. For almost two
hundred years evangelical churches have held planned
evangelistic campaigns. In British countries they are called
"missions." Typically in North America they have been
called "revival meetings." Today the terms more in favor
are meetings for "renewal," or Bible conferences, or
deeper life conventions. Whatever they are called, they are
generally for a predetermined duration, planned well in
advance, highly advertised (or should be), buttressed by
special singing and musical attractions, and marked most
of all by the presence of a visiting evangelist.

The best known endeavors of this type are the Billy
Graham Crusades, which have been instrumental in
reaching thousands for Christ. Such city-wide campaigns
have been very fruitful with many other evangelists also.
Usually holiness churches have cooperated, sometimes
prominently. The religious and moral tone of entire cities
has been markedly cleansed and strengthened by such
events.

VALUES IN PLANNED REVIVALS

But how should we view planned revival endeavors at the local church level? That they are now more difficult is undeniable, due to TV, the fast pace of modern life, and the materialistic mood which leaves people spiritually unconcerned. The sight of a big sign, REVIVAL, in front of a church does not excite the public as it once did. Time was when such a meeting was the only new thing happening, and people flocked to revival because they had nothing more interesting to do. Those days are gone forever. Attracting attention, creating interest, and getting people in is today a much more difficult and demanding challenge.

In view of the small returns experienced by many churches still clinging precariously to this traditional activity, is this any longer a viable mode of evangelism? To this question several answers may be given. In principle, the need for such special efforts arises out of the tendency of spirituality in the average church to decline. Some special effort is needed to awaken the church and spark new commitment and vitality. Then for a while a new plateau of blessing and fruitfulness is enjoyed. But sooner or later the tide will ebb. When a woman protested to the famous Presbyterian evangelist E. J. Bulgin, "I don't believe in revivals; they don't last," he retorted, "Neither does a bath; but I hope you take one once in a while." The fact that no matter how successful the revival campaign is the church will still need another in a few months does not prove that holding such meetings is futile.

A further observation is that there is freshness in a new voice, a new personality, and a new way of doing things that blows a few cobwebs away and lets in breezes of new air. The visiting preacher may articulate the same truths the pastor has been hammering on for months, but an unconscious but increasing deafness, caused by famil- iarity, kept his people from hearing; now it sounds brand new, and they find their way to an altar for pardon or purity. Of course if the pastor is small-minded and jealous, and can't take this, he had better not call evangelists. But in this case he gives himself away, revealing that to him the protection of his ego is more important than the spiritual progress of his people.

Too much should not be made of the basic agree- ment between the pastor's preaching and the evangelist's. Although the same doctrines may be enunciated, God- called evangelists typically have a unique ministry that enriches the life of the church. Theirs may be a specialty in some delicate area, perhaps family relations; or rare skill in uncovering wounds and sores that eluded the pastor. Sometimes listeners will accept searching truth from a stranger which they would tend to resent from their pastor. He knows them, and they know he knows them, but the evangelist does not, which removes from their minds any suspicion that he is preaching "at" them. They are thus more receptive to the truth. Other things being equal, churches will always be stronger for the deeper roots that grow in a short revival meeting.

The implication of this is that where there has been preparatory prayer, where truth is preached under the anointing of the Spirit, and where the effort is buttressed by the personal holiness of everyone on the platform (including singers), total failure is impossible. Some victories will be won, even if not at the altar, that will move the church further up the road. It is a poor effort indeed that does no good at all.

And for statistics—who is to say what constitutes a big meeting and a small? How can the salvation of one child be measured in monetary terms? There have been some spectacular campaigns with altars lined every night, yet comparatively little to point to six weeks later. In contrast there have been some very modest efforts which did not (in the view of mercenary critics) seem "cost effective" but which produced preachers, missionaries, and set loose a chain of "small" influences that rolled on in revival momentum for months.

It must also be conceded that seldom does a planned campaign explode into the *revival* that the people have prayed for and that the pastor longs for. But this degree of failure is no ground for discouragement or for abandoning such planned efforts. I knew one pastor who managed to persuade his people to cooperate with him in three two-week campaigns almost back-to-back—with one or two weeks rest in between—and whereas hardly a hand was turned in the first two meetings a real revival broke out in the third, which revolutionized the church and precipitated a surge of rapid growth. The pastor believed the first two campaigns were necessary preparations for the third.

A yet further value in planned campaigns is the bonding and unifying effect of an intense and highly concentrated focus of activity at the church. For this brief period of time the entire congregation directs its attention to the house of God and the special activity there. Even those who do not attend are aware of what is going on, which in itself is a powerful stimulus to the conscience. Those who faithfully participate are benefited, if by nothing else, by the discipline, self-denial, planning, organizing, and general effort put forth to be present. Children become more church-conscious, adults are compelled to reassess their priorities, and the entire body benefits by the new flow of fellowship and mutual joy— even burden—which being together in church every night creates.

MAKING OUR CAMPAIGNS MORE EFFECTIVE

Yet with all these arguments in favor of the planned campaign, it must be admitted that some of them seem more disappointing and barren than they should; and sometimes there seems to be validity in the wonder on the part of board members if perhaps there might be a more effective method of outreach for the dollars invested. After all, it does cost a lot these days to hire an evangelist and music team. Therefore, if we are not willing to abandon the traditional planned revival campaign, are there ways we can make them more effective?

1. Let the pastor and his evangelism committee decide well in advance the type of meeting they need—for the building up of the church or for outreach. These types of meetings are radically different, calling for different kinds of speakers and different musical attractions. Some pastors want at least once a year a holiness convention or Bible convention type of revival, and call a teaching evangelist. The aim will be to foster revival within the church by careful instruction in holiness. The focus will be on the reclamation of backsliders, the resolution of spiritual problems in the church, the stabilizing of families, and the sanctification of believers. Probing truth will be preached, but also large amounts of encouragement, instruction, and faith building.

Then these pastors want at least one other campaign to be beamed to the outsider, and they put in place a different set of plans. Advertising is different, preparatory prayer is different, organized effort among their people for bringing unsaved people in is different. This is a more complicated and more difficult endeavor—but it can be promoted successfully (and will not require any more overall expenditure of energy, thought, and skill than either the survey or telemarketing).

2. Next in order is the selection of evangelists. Wrong judgment here will nullify the best of plans. Not every evangelist will go over in every type of church. Pastors need to know their community and their church. Usually calling an evangelist on hearsay is risky. Furthermore, the Big Name evangelist is not always suitable for a small or mid-size church. In many cases the lesser known but experienced, proved, solid, dependable, praying man or woman, who is not loaded with stunts and gimmicks (and has only holiness books to sell); who has common sense, understands pastoral problems, is courteous both in and out of the pulpit, and who is sufficiently learned and refined not to embarrass intelligent listeners, *and* can preach a warm, intelligent, well-crafted sermon that is biblical and to the point—such persons will be more constructive than a platform fireball who can create excitement that intellectually and spiritually is largely visceral.

Unfortunately, it occasionally happens that an unwise evangelist makes more enemies and raises more dust and spreads more confusion than the poor pastor can undo in a year. Such a pastor may not be blamed if he is tempted to join the ranks of no-revival pastors. But this would be an overreaction. The wiser course is simply to be more sure of one's man or woman the next time.

Although God-called, full-time evangelists should be used, at times the need of a local church can best be met by a fellow-pastor who has evangelistic gifts, or a professor or general official.

3. Much prayer and thought should be invested in deciding on a date. Naturally, to some extent this will be determined by the evangelist. Whether to take a poor date in order to get a particular evangelist, or accept a less

preferred evangelist in order to secure a good date is a question to which different answers might be given. This comment might be in order: Any date is a good one if God comes on the scene. I have known successful revivals that were held in summer, in irrigating season, in hunting season, in snowy winter weather. If search for the perfect date prevents a church from launching out, they will never venture, for the perfect date will never be found. And if the church settles on what to them is the best date, chances are ten to one that the evangelist the church wants already has that date booked!

4. Preparations that a church puts into a planned campaign will have much more to do with its success than will dates or even the choice of evangelists (assuming basic soundness). Some rules of thumb are:

a. *Talk up the meeting* at least three months in advance. The coming event should be kept before the people constantly, from the pulpit, in the bulletin, in weekly mailings, with upbeat, enthusiastic promotion, until anticipation inevitably builds up to fever pitch.

However, don't oversell the evangelist. Keep his name before the people but ration the palaver. If the people are assured that he is the greatest speaker they have ever heard and the wisest, and they come the first night expecting a seven-day-wonder only to find him quite ordinary, an emotional setback will have been given to the meeting from which recovery may prove impossible.

b. *Involve as many people as possible* in the preparatory process. If the pastor is the sole public relations person and does all the leg work, the people will not only let him but approach the meeting languidly, if they attend at all. They need to become emotionally involved before the meeting begins. If they have been serving on committees—prayer, advertising, ushering, hospitality, transportation, home calling, music—they will come to feel that this is their meeting and its success will be their success. There is nothing equaling a sense of responsibility to bring out the best performance in church members.

c. *Multiply prayer meetings.* Not one or two hurriedly arranged a few days before the evangelist arrives, but dozens, at the church, in private homes, in the daytime, evenings. This should be going on weeks in advance. We should learn from the Billy Graham campaigns. Advance managers move into a community; in the case of a major campaign, a year in advance. The first and most important thing they do is set up hundreds of prayer meetings all over the city. Many qualities about these campaigns contribute to their effectiveness, but the mysterious power that draws people by the hundreds out of their seats night after night, to go forward publicly, is undoubtedly more traceable to those months of prayer than all the other features combined.

I have never seen significant results without an intense prayer preparation. In one city I had but one Sunday to give to a church. The location was impossible—a huge public school gym with about fifty folding chairs on concrete in the center of that vast area. Every move of every chair sounded either like a rifle crack or a chain saw. The miserable acoustics made speaking difficult. But five adults knelt at the improvised altar for salvation. I understood when I learned that the little struggling group had met in cottage prayer meetings every night the previous week, including Saturday night.

d. *Clear the decks.* This is necessary to make room for the special prayer meetings, for one thing. The average church calendar is dense with activities: athletic events, parties, children's activities, choir practices, committee meetings, discipling classes, youth and adult retreats, Bible quizzing, cantata rehearsal. How can even prayer meetings be squeezed into such a packed program? Which events can be modified or suspended to make room for the new prayer push? If there is no adjustment, the praying people will be worn out before the meeting starts.

It will not be good strategy publicly to take the position that the prayer meetings can be attended by the elderly and others not otherwise occupied. This, of course, is what actually occurs in most churches—but the meager results indict the policy. Some way the pastor must persuade the board or council to commit themselves to a policy which suspends or postpones some activities. All of these activities are important to the usual calendar of the church. But there comes a time, by some temporary adjustments in the schedule, when the board must set its values in order of priority, and decide whether having a real revival is important enough to make room for it.

As important as adjustment is before the campaign, it is doubly mandatory during the campaign. More than one meeting has been scuttled by failure here. The church operates as usual with all the normal activities, and the result is that *some* of these busy lay folk manage to get to a few services to hear the visiting speaker. Apparently they expect him to bring revival in his suitcase. I have actually known revival campaigns to be held when the young people were away at a retreat, long-planned social events were determinedly held, and cantata rehearsals commandeered much of the time and energy. In one case, over a hundred people were in the sanctuary practicing while the "revival" had to be chucked into a basement room. As long as pastors and churches permit this sort of diffusion of interests and scattering of attention, treating the revival as (pardon the expression) something "the cat dragged in," they needn't expect God's blessing. They are wasting good money and the evangelist's time. Such fiascos shout poor planning and poor management.

This saying is credited to John Wesley: "Fanaticism is

expecting results without giving due attention to adequate causes." Into what category, then, shall we place the pastor who permits his church to sink hundreds of dollars into a campaign for which he has not thoroughly prepared?

e. Finally, the church needs to have *developed a prospect awareness.* For months preparatory evangelism should be carried on in anticipation of the forthcoming campaign. This should include friendship evangelism, hospitality evangelism, personal witnessing, literature seed-sowing. Prayer meetings should focus on the salvation needs of real persons for whom church members are carrying a genuine burden. The advance prayer meetings should not be permitted to be preempted by Uncle Joe's asthma or Aunt Sally's flu. Such needs dominate the prayers of the typical church group all year. There surely should be one season when the prayer warriors are permitted to intercede for the lost. This is not hardheartedness or indifference to the physical needs and financial problems of people, but it is a declaration that more urgent concerns claim our attention right now.

This kind of praying combined with the various outreach activities that have been going on will bring into the sphere of the campaign a large number of people already under conviction, upon whom the Spirit is already moving, who are already responding to the love and interest of this church. There should be a loving web of influences which the Holy Spirit has to work with. There will be if there has been in the life of the church what some have called the right mix of evangelistic activities.

WHEN "REVIVAL" BECOMES REVIVAL

There are purists who insist that the word *revival* should be restricted to what happens to the church, while *evangelism* should be the term used to designate an outreach campaign. However, the history of "revivals" describes great powerful movements of the Spirit that revive the church and sweep hundreds of sinners into the kingdom almost simultaneously. Sometimes these historic revivals occur with little advance planning or organizing. At other times they erupt out of campaigns that start out as very ordinary. Naturally, every church and pastor hope that the campaign they are about to launch will prove to be such a demonstration of divine power. When this happens rapid church growth normally follows for months, sometimes years; and because it is God's work it will be easier to mold and disciple the converts.

Churches that experience profound revival never forget it. They are almost immediately propelled to a higher level of spiritual energy and a deeper grounding in spiritual values. Such revival provides a standard by which children, youth, and adults come to measure all religious activities thereafter. When restlessness seeps into a church, and praying people feel uneasy, it just might be not the fermentation of a critical spirit, but a memory— and a longing. There is validity in the cliché, "I was born in the fire, and I can't be happy in the smoke."

As a teenager, I witnessed a spiritual movement that touched as altar seekers some five hundred people. It began after weeks of special prayer meetings of teenagers, and as the courageous faith-action of a lay woman who simply announced one Sunday night that a tent meeting would begin Thursday night. She had no tent, no benches, no hymnals, no evangelist, and there was no advertising—ever. But when we sauntered over to the announced location on Thursday evening, we found a tent set up and people crowding in; three nights later a second tent had to be added. The double tent was packed every night for weeks. People came—without advertising—

from a radius of fifty miles. The laywoman's husband led a bit of singing, exhorted a little, and people swarmed to the altar. When they began to testify, another group lined the long altar. It was a spiritual turning point in my life as well as in the lives of many others. Becoming an unbeliever would be difficult if not impossible for those of us who witnessed firsthand such a degree of God's power.

In contrast, sometimes a set, planned campaign sparks the overspreading flames. This was the case with the revival of 1972 that began in Saskatoon, Saskatchewan, and swept across Canada and dipped into the States. The evangelists carried out their commitment, then left, but not before they became aware of a spiritual prairie fire. The movement transcended denominational lines, mended homes, re-fired churches, and was characterized by spontaneous all-night services. The four pastors most immediately in the vanguard testified that it was fundamentally a holiness revival—with an emphasis on confessing sin, making restitution, putting all on the altar, and asking for and claiming the fullness of the Holy Spirit.[1]

Yet lesser revivals are not to be scorned. A revival can be genuine and life-changing which does not reach such spectacular proportions. Let a pastor and his people therefore invest all they have in the planned campaign and be thankful for even limited showers of blessing. Some hearts will be revived. Some chronic seekers will become grounded. Some problems will be solved. Some floundering new or young Christian will receive just the light he needs and will go on with renewed commitment and assurance. All things being equal, the churches that refuse to give up on the revival campaign but continue to make a place for it in their annual planning will not only grow in numbers but develop in strength and depth as viable holiness churches.[2]

Part Three
DIMENSIONS IN NURTURING

11

GROWING STURDY SAINTS

D iscipling converts is perhaps the most challenging part of the ministry. There is a kind of pastoral personality, which when combined with an exciting program, can draw people in. It requires skills at a much deeper level to establish them in the Lord after they have been reached. At this level a pastor's perception of needs, his understanding of people, his theological grasp, his teaching abilities are tested to the limit.

While discipling includes assimilating new people into the social and organic structure of the church, this is not its real center. Developing loyal and informed church members is important, but neither is that the supreme goal. Knowing God is the supreme goal. People can be absorbed into the life of the church—in fact can become very active—without becoming deep and strong in the things of God. They can even be helped by the ministries of the church to mature into emotionally balanced and healthy persons—all without a profoundly intimate "I-Thou" walk with God. Therefore, if after five years the new member is a busy churchman yet still spiritually superficial, the discipling process has miscarried. As important as fellowship is, it is eclipsed by the need to learn to pray.

It is up to the pastor to devise a program which has maximum exposure to God as its deliberate objective. The pastoral assignment is nothing less than helping Christians "grow up in all aspects into Him, who is the head, even Christ" (Eph. 4:15, NASB). The goal is sturdy saints: established, mature, exemplary, and reliable men and women of God.

Let us see if we can understand how the pastor can be effective in contributing to this goal.

SPIRITUAL REQUISITES

In the Convert

Sickly spiritual babes will require an extra amount of attention, and even with the best of care may not make it. Which is to say that the pastor's success will depend not only on his own skills but on the basic attitude of the young Christian. A sound, radical conversion grounded in deep repentance will predispose a person to an enthusiastic responsiveness to guidance. Such a convert is turned on to spiritual activities, and eagerly wants to be at the heart of things. The convert is more apt to adjust his schedule to attend Bible studies, prayer meetings, and church services than some of the older members. He is borne along by the excitement and joy of his first love. This of course is the pastor's grand opening. Let him seize this springtime of the soul and cultivate faithfully this newly turned, receptive soil.

There is no substitute for the new birth. No amount of tender loving care can make a saint out of an unregenerate sinner. The substance of spiritual life, implanted by the Holy Spirit, must be present. Some people become religious, even with great gusto and zeal, who do not yet know Christ. They have mistaken conviction for conversion and reformation for salvation. Worst of all they have mistaken emotional relief for a changed heart. But soon their glamorous new religion will turn sour and they will drift away. God have mercy on the church whose pastor has no discernment in these matters.

But even when conversion has been real, persons vary in their responsiveness to discipling. Basic spiritual capacities greatly differ. Some folk will get to heaven who on earth will never be so deeply spiritual as others. Diverse temperaments dictate diverse ways of relating to spiritual reality, including emotional reactions and inclinations. Some are doers. They must keep active. Being quiet, even to meditate, is difficult for them. Deep reading and study is an unknown art. Others are introvertive and thoughtful. The study sessions will appeal to them, but not the house calling. These differences will affect not only respective styles of Christian service but also growing pace. Some will hop on the fast express while others get there by and by on the slow freight.

Those who tend by nature to be easily discouraged, timid, backward, perhaps sluggish will need special care. And all will need close attention during the early stages of spiritual infancy. Barnabas exhorted the new Antioch Christians that "with purpose of heart they would cleave unto the Lord" (Acts 11:23, KJV). Beneath the personality and temperamental differences the strength of a convert's purpose is the all-important key to future growth. Pastors will search for ways to help the convert reconfirm and deepen this purpose.

In the Environment

A spiritually dull atmosphere will produce nominal Christians. They will be aware of no high standard by which they can acquire a biblical perception of normality. If church life revolves around social activities, young Christians will be conditioned to a religious life which majors on food, fun, and games. Not that this side of church life has no place, but it should be subordinate not dominant.

A church, on the other hand, that is intensely alive spiritually, that has vibrant worship services, frequent altar services, exciting testimony meetings, spine-tingling song services, numerous prayer meetings, anointed preaching, and real revivals will constitute a rich environment for growth. Converts will thrive in such a setting. They will breathe deeply of spiritual reality and learn to think in terms of a high standard. They will never thereafter be satisfied with a dead church.

THE INCORPORATING PROCESS

Confirmed Confidence

If people are to be rooted in this particular church and grappled to this pastor, the confidence painfully and slowly gained in the "reaching" process must be confirmed. Too many times, when converts get on the inside and watch for a while, confidence is eroded, if not destroyed.

It is easy to say that converts must be attached to Jesus, not to people. Of course. But they come to Jesus through people, and for a long time people will be their models and their support. They will learn how to follow Jesus by watching the ones who brought them to the Lord. Infants have to be carried before they can walk, and they toddle before they run. They don't enter a marathon the day after they are born. Yes, new Christians must learn to stand on their own feet, but let us not take the steadying hands away too soon.

Two perils are especially critical during the opening months of a new person's involvement with the church. One is the discovery that all is not lovely in Zion. Sometimes this is no more than the warts of our humanity, but a shock nevertheless to idealistic converts who supposed that the church should be heavenly. As Wesley Tracy says, "We forget that the family is often the focus of friction. And when the church has a typical family conflict, new converts and naïve believers may think that they have become the victims of yet another 'bait and switch.'"[1]

In some churches the conflict may be much more serious than surface warts. The power structure may be carnally controlled. There may be undercurrents of rivalry and bickering, backbiting and gossip; even immorality may be lurking in the shadows. The discovery of this seamy side can be devastating to an idealistic young Christian. The mature saints must gather around the wounded member and help him or her through this spiritual trauma.

The other peril is equally dangerous and more subtle. It is the convert's discovery that all the "love" and concern lavished on him to *win* him was only a means to an end. It was not real. He was not loved for himself but simply seen as one more cog in the wheel of church growth. All-out attention shifts too quickly to new prospects, who will be overwhelmed with attention until won, when it will shift again to someone else. This is the greatest crisis in the confirmation of confidence.

Converts will not last, or at least ever be strong, unless the confidence that brought them into the church is reinforced all along the line. It is of paramount necessity that as they watch the pastor at close range they become increasingly convinced that he is a good man, a real man of God, in whom they can trust. This knowledge will buoy them, inspire them, sturdy them. Then they must come to see that this really *is* a caring church, with deep, genuine, dependable love. When they are thoroughly convinced of this, they will imbibe the same love, and more and more be capable of pouring it out on others.

Involvement—With Care

New Christians need to feel that they belong. This aspect of incorporation depends not only on the pastor but upon the ability of the "ins" to open their arms and draw the new ones into their circles. In every way possible they should be given a chance to participate. This extends to social activities, athletic (if there are such), nursing home teams, music if qualified, home Bible studies, flower committee, or whatever form of activity can be opened to them, within the range of their skills and interests.

Also every effort should be made to get them to missionary meetings, zone rallies, camp meetings, and other events which will expose them to the larger family. This will give them perspective. The inspiration factor in these larger affairs will excite and stimulate their spiritual life and in the process their knowledge of their new church connection will broaden. In many cases, it is in these meetings that the new convert finds his way to the altar for entire sanctification.

But a peril is too much too soon. An eager new Christian wants to be in church every time the door opens. He is game to try almost anything. But the pastor must be alert to extreme hyperactivity, which inevitably will bring physical exhaustion with its emotional letdown. Furthermore, if the convert has family responsibilities, too much too fast can complicate relationships with unsaved spouses or children, who may already be feeling resentful about the sudden shift of time, interest, and attention.

Doubly perilous is the all too common tendency to try to tie new people to the church by electing them to major office. New converts should be drawn into the life of the church without premature responsibility for running the church. "Not a new convert," says Paul about elders (1 Tim. 3:6, NASB). The proscription is equally sound for board members and Sunday school teachers. Learning habits of faithful attendance, of tithing, sharing the secondary responsibilities should come well ahead of membership on the church board or council. Especially should pastors go slowly if they see signs of undue itchiness for elective office. Failure to exercise caution here has resulted too often in disaster for the Christian and embarrassment for the church.[2]

In one of my pastorates, an especially talented and enthusiastic woman was made president of the missionary society—too soon after becoming a church member. It was a traumatic year for her. At the end of the year she said, "I'm not ready for this kind of responsibility yet. I need time to pray and study the Bible, to become acquainted with my Lord and the church." She was wiser than her mentor. Later she stepped in with steadiness and grace, and for many years has served the church well in numerous local and district offices. But we came close to losing her that year.

A similar mistake in handling new converts, often with tragic consequences, is making celebrities out of converts who are impressive "catches" or whose conversion is especially dramatic. We emblazon them with limelight, and trot them here and there to give their testimonies. Unless thoroughly sanctified—not likely at this stage—they will almost inevitably become vain and self-centered in their "ministry," and may never be able to shake their addiction to public attention and adulation. They may even launch out into half-baked "ministries" before they are spiritually deep enough to know what ministry means. "Lest he become conceited" is the second half of Paul's admonition.

Encouraging new converts to testify in church and seek to win their friends to Christ is one thing. Using them as advertising decoys for the church is quite another.

Therefore the sum of the matter is this: That pastor is wise who draws new converts immediately into a discipling class, where they are learners more than doers. A proper discipling program requires commitment to large blocks of time over a period of six months to a year. The new Christian should not be expected to juggle this extensive study program in competition with a lot of other duties. Let this one thing absorb his major thought and energy. If this program is followed, he will be worth much more to the church later on.

12

THE DYNAMICS OF GROWTH

In the task of growing sturdy saints it is essential that the pastor understand thoroughly the dynamics of growth. Growth is a process requiring both time and experience. Maturity is not a supernatural, instantaneous gift in the sense that forgiveness and cleansing are. It is an acquirement that involves the inner maturation of the person plus the understanding that accrues from daily living. We have to experience adversity to understand adversity. We must experience disappointment to learn how to handle disappointment. We must experience sorrow to know how to bear sorrow. We must struggle with time—pressures, work, schedules, multiple calls for our attention—if we are going to learn how to master time. We must "grow up" as persons if we are to "grow up" spiritually.

TYPICAL STAGES

New Christians, especially the whole-souled kind, are very apt to go through stages.

1. At first they are gripped by the *excitement of*

novelty. Everything is new—their feelings, their outlook, their expectations, their values, their circle of associates, where they go. Being a Christian is for them a grand adventure.

2. The next stage may be the *optimism of fervency*. Faith is not only childlike but naïve. It is all-encompassing and accepts no limits to the power of prayer and the possibilities of what "we" can do.

3. Stage Two is beautiful, but it is apt to be followed by *the excesses of fanaticism*. This is an extremely dangerous period in the young Christian's pilgrimage. For in this stage he typically wants instant and huge results. He attempts heroic but unrealistic enterprises. He may fast to an excessive extent. He may plunge into Christian work far beyond either his physical strength or his natural abilities. He may give away his resources unwisely. He may neglect his health and forget that he has a body. He is too eager to win the world to have time to settle down into the humdrum of a discipleship class. His fervor has become fever. In this stage he is highly vulnerable to some cultic aberration which promises even more spectacular power. For some, the tongues emphasis may have strong appeal because it seems so "spiritual."

4. The next stage is often the *furor of imperiousness*. As he looks around he becomes aware of the snail's pace of the church, and so he begins to attempt to set things right. He scolds and taunts, accusing others of laziness and indifference.

5. Sooner or later this will be followed by the *depression of reaction*. Having worn himself out physically and drained himself emotionally, and discovered that Jericho walls don't always fall flat, the convert begins to withdraw. He may withdraw into himself, becoming as silent as he was previously verbose—discouraged with

both himself and the church. The peril now is the likelihood of drifting into a censorious spirit.

What is the relation of all of this to the need for entire sanctification? It is all part of a spiritual/human continuum. Without understanding what is happening, the believer struggles to find himself as a Christian, and the struggle is a mixture of normal immaturity compounded by a religious willfulness, the true quality of which he has not yet seen. He is not aware that much of his zeal is in the energy of the flesh. It is only as he discovers the Big I in his fervent thrashings for the Lord, gets to the end of himself, and seeks and finds purity of heart that he will enter into rest.

6. So the sixth stage (it is hoped), is *the quiet strength of sanctified stability*. Self is subdued. Love takes over. Trust finds a new level. The demanding, imperious spirit is stilled. Humility replaces pride and self-importance. Inner peace replaces feverish striving.

The wise pastor therefore will seek to understand the stages through which his people are passing. He will try to know how they are thinking and what their need is at this point. He will seek to avoid pushing beyond their capacity, remembering the words of Jesus to his unsanctified disciples, "I have yet many things to say unto you, but ye cannot bear them now" (John 16:12, KJV). Jesus knew that a mighty baptism with the Spirit would open their spiritual eyes and expand their capacities exponentially. But meanwhile pastoral care had to adjust to present reality.

However, this should never become ground for avoiding holiness preaching, on the rationale that "my people are not ready yet." The Holy Spirit will use clear, strong holiness preaching as His prime tool to get them ready. But the pastor will be patient and understanding when his preaching seems to fall on deaf ears. If he keeps close to his converts personally and continues to preach lovingly, sooner or later a light will come on, truth will be grasped, need will be seen, and the Christian will move up to a new spiritual level. Someone has wisely advised, "Hold the lamp of truth high, so people can see. Don't dash it in their faces—that will not help them to see." Preach faithfully but not pugnaciously.

THE PLACE OF DISCIPLINE

The dynamics of growth include the struggle to become a disciplined person. This, as even the entirely sanctified person must learn, is endemic to true maturity. This is the follow-through requisite for personal growth. Unless sanctification is followed by discipline it will be lost. While only God can confirm and deepen sanctification, He will do it by means of the Christian's resolute adoption of the disciplines of daily Christian living.

It bears repeating: only discipline will achieve the ongoing, day-by-day conditions necessary for sanctification's preservation. In sanctification a soul is thoroughly adjusted to divine priorities. These priorities are prayer, Bible, church, soul-winning, stewardship. Such priorities are adopted, indeed, *internalized,* as the very structure of life. The heart acquiesces with a glad yes.

But it takes more than goodwill to implement these priorities consistently day after day. It takes rigorous self-control and self-direction. This is true because life does not make it easy to practice our priorities. Life is made up of people, family, jobs, duties, events, appointments, bills, sicknesses, the unexpected—always the unexpected. Life never behaves quite as we should like it to. And everything that happens is pushing our time plan into odd shapes, injecting new vectors of influence and direction.

As a result, our priorities get jostled, maybe even momentarily obscured from view. Unless discipline comes to the rescue, our priorities are in jeopardy; but whatever jeopardizes our basic Christian patterns jeopardizes our holy relationship with God.

Not that God holds us in a straightjacket. Flexibility in personal schedules, even in devotions, is no sin. Indeed, it can be occasioned by our very sanctified service, for as we are led by the Spirit we will give attention to the unexpected invasions of people-need. But a disciplined Christian will always be on guard lest people and events gradually pry him away from a lifestyle that is structured by prayer and the church. How quickly and subtly even the good can become the enemy of the best.

The pastor who would grow sturdy saints must demonstrate that he himself is a disciplined person. His people will quickly stumble onto the truth here. If he is undisciplined, they will soon become aware of his gorging at potlucks, unbridled talkativeness, excessive freedom with his hands around women, disorganized work habits, excessive time off, careless appearance, sloppy stance in the pulpit, lounging on the platform, irritability in board meetings, illiterate speech, inordinate depression when reverses come, and all such weaknesses—which, unfortunately, some pastors exhibit. Somehow their talk about discipline lacks credibility. If, therefore, he would help his young and immature Christians become strong and disciplined persons, he had better begin with himself. Demonstrated discipline illustrates principles and lends wings to one's words.

But assuming that the pastor is a good example, he should include in his preaching and discipling classes a large measure of attention to this vital fact of Christian life and character.

The points of discipline most urgently needed by young converts are:

1. Self-control—of emotions, appetites, impulses, speech, and spending.
2. Structure—the achievement of some degree of orderliness and plan in one's life, as opposed to haphazardness.
3. Steadiness—the mastery of the art of moving forward dependably in our tasks in spite of lethargic feelings. A mature Christian lives by principle, not by impulse or emotion. This applies even to religious assurance. Matthew Henry said, "When I cannot live by the faith of assurance I will live by the faith of adherence."

SPIRITUAL FORMATION

Today Christian growth has become a discipling specialty called Spiritual Formation. It is a new term for Protestants and a fresh emphasis on an old concept. Careless habits, learned attitudes, distorted perceptions, lifelong prejudices, spending patterns, and such elements of personal character acquired while in sin are deeply ingrained in a new Christian even after sin, as such, has been put away. It takes a while for these patterns to be perceived as spiritual issues. Paul said, "Continue to work out your salvation with fear and trembling" (Phil. 2:12), by which he meant to translate inner holiness into visible practice, experience into ethics, intentions into performance. And in the process forge a strong Christian character.

The Christian must learn to think like a Christian (Rom. 12:2).[1] The conscience needs to be educated. Spiritual formation should be marked by a growing sensitivity to and discernment of the Good, the Beautiful, and the True. The training of our aesthetic tastes will make us more attractive and well-rounded Christians. Emotional life should be cultivated in the direction of deeper feelings about things that matter, greater compassion toward human need, capacity for anger against evil, and moderation in expression. Feelings may be intense but need to be under control.[2]

Spiritual formation includes a progressive grasp of the implications of stewardship. The person who has for years spent thoughtlessly on trinkets and luxuries must grow out of such childishness, and discover the elevated joys of diverting his material resources to the kingdom of God. This is a process which may need the guidance of a wise pastor and fellow lay persons, but most of all will depend upon the deliberateness and intelligence with which the convert gives himself to it.

Growing sturdy saints therefore will require from a pastor a large amount of pastoral attention, in and out of the pulpit. Continuous pressure and guidance are needed toward the formation of established habits that form the framework of one's lifestyle. Watchfulness of attitudes, carefulness to maintain commitments, and deliberate renewal of enthusiasms are all essential to spiritual formation. Understanding is especially important in three areas:

1. Spiritual formation will drift into mere humanistic self-improvement unless the Christian acquires an understanding of what it means to walk in the Spirit (Gal. 5:25) and learns to do it. Keeping in step with the Spirit requires learning to recognize His signals. Coming to detect His promptings and His restraints is central to everything in the Christian life. This includes the discernment between true Spirit-impressions and those that come from other sources. Yet the Christian who is in the process of learning to know the Spirit intimately must be warned

frequently against the peril of pride and independence, as if he now had a private line to God which exempts him from the need for human teachers.

2. Some perception of the difference between carnality (as delineated in 1 Cor. 3) and humanity (both "normal" and marred) is essential, or the Christian will be insecure in his relationship to God, and unsure of his own spiritual state.

3. The growing Christian needs to understand the crucial nature of the acute pressure points which arise in his life from time to time. These include friction or misunderstanding with another person; a discovery of an unChristlike spirit which has hurt another and which needs to be confessed; a reminder by the Spirit of an item of restitution which still needs attention; an urge to undertake a task for the Lord, which we are absolutely sure we can't do and which frightens us; a leading to speak to a friend or neighbor about his or her spiritual need; a challenge by the Spirit to take some unusual step of faith in stewardship; an inner nudge to make some special adjustment in lifestyle, perhaps respecting dress, our TV viewing, or the stories we tell; a personal hurt received at the hands of another, which threatens to rob us of our joy and plunge us into a self-nursing mood; an adjustment to our spouse or other family members, which God is talking to us about.

The important thing here which the Christian simply must see is that any one of these pressure points can be pivotal to further progress or incipient regression.[3] They cannot be ignored or bypassed, or driven underground into our subconscious, no matter how painful the issue may be. To attempt to do so is fatal. But every time such a crisis is faced and resolved God's way we have won a victory, we are stronger, and the cause of spiritual formation is pushed miles up the road.

The pastor's tools will be:

1. Quiet example—especially under pressure.

2. Personal conversation in a warm and nonthreatening setting wherein the Christian's soul can gently be probed, his relapses faced, his problems isolated.

3. Study groups where attention is focused on spiritual formation. As is well known, Wesley's secret in the nurture of his converts was the class meetings and the bands. "In Wesley's eye," writes A. Skevington Wood, "[the class meeting] was the keystone of the entire Methodist edifice."[4] It was the "disciplinary unit of the society."

4. The circulation—perhaps followed by discussion—of devotional books. A pastor should know the books he recommends, and judiciously match the book to the person. And let him be aware of the doctrinal slant. All devotional writing has a doctrinal orientation, even that which claims not to. Aberrant viewpoints will creep in here and there, very subtly, and the unwary beginner will be unconsciously shaped in his thinking in ways not intended by his Wesleyan pastor.

A new Christian cannot be expected to discern such matters, but he has a right to assume that his pastor is a competent and safe guide.

5. The clear teaching and preaching of God's sanctifying grace as the central catalyst in the spiritual formation process. More of this in the following chapter.

13

SHEPHERDING TOWARD HEART HOLINESS

The ultimately defeating obstacle to sturdy saintliness will be the remains of sin in the believer. Let not the Wesleyan pastor forget the doctrine that we are born with a sinful twist in our nature constituting an abnormal proneness toward aversion to God and to self-idolatry; that regeneration subdues this aversion but does not uproot it and that this remaining self-centeredness will compete with the new loyalty, causing a crippling and debilitating doublemindedness. This will constitute an abnormal proneness to negative reaction in the face of disappointment and disillusionment.

So far such doctrine is just basic orthodoxy, whether Wesleyan, Lutheran, or Calvinist. But Wesleyans (and some Calvinists) believe that God can cleanse the Christian's heart of this doublemindedness and fill it with the Holy Spirit as the Great Enabler. Unless the believer is led into this experience, his growth before long will begin to stall, for the essence of the carnal mind is a reluctance to accept the full implications of the lordship of Jesus. The convert in the flush of his new joy and life-orientation is unaware—or at least only dimly aware—of this inner reluctance. But as time goes on the excitement will subside, disillusionments will come, new light will dawn to open up a whole spectrum of demands in stewardship and obedience not foreseen, and the Christian will find himself beginning to struggle. Latent rebelliousness, self-will, personal ambitions, materialism, and lusts will all begin to ferment and cast a shadow over his spiritual life. Gradually a battle royal will develop, ultimately reaching an acute crisis of wills.

At this point the Christian will, if he is to go on—reach a crossroads of total surrender, at a level and concerning issues never even thought of at the time of conversion. Self will be decisively dethroned. If this crisis is not resolved on the side of heart holiness, he will either drift back into the world or settle into a nominal churchianity, having a "form of godliness but denying its power" (2 Tim. 3:5). His progress toward becoming a sturdy saint will have been aborted. But if he faces the challenge of the carnal self-life and the full will of God for him, and be willing to go all-out for God's best, be a true steward of all he is and has, and become thoroughly spiritually-minded, with an intensified and concentrated devotion to Christ, he will then be on the way to his full potential. The pastor will watch him grow with joy and satisfaction. Which means that the pastor can grow sturdy saints best by leading his converts into holiness.

Does it need to be added that the most successful pastor in leading Christians into Canaan and developing sturdy saints is the pastor who models best. If he is a man of prayer, lives in the Spirit, experiences daily God-given insight and guidance, and is obviously blessed in his soul, it will be natural for young Christians to feel at home with that kind of religion. Biblical spirituality is caught more easily than taught.

THE URGENCY OF INDOCTRINATION

But that sentence does not mean that teaching doctrine can be dispensed with if only the pastor is saintly enough. If he is saintly enough, he will want to teach, for his very love for his people will incite him to impart to them the truth.

Normally, sound conversion sparks an intellectual awakening. People who before floated in an intellectual vacuum find themselves with a new desire to learn. Especially do they desire to acquire a knowledge of the Bible and of what they are supposed to believe. So they ask questions and attend classes. This is the time for the alert pastor to guide them into a meaningful reading program. For many the level must be very elementary, or they will become bewildered and discouraged.

The pastor himself should lead the way as teacher. His sermons should be instructive. He should be prepared to answer questions and discuss difficulties in his pastoral calling (cf. Acts 20:20). He should conduct discipling classes, and not be too quick to shift this ministry to lay persons, few of whom are really qualified. Of course developing qualified teachers among the laity, who can handle doctrinal and ethical subjects competently, should be a goal of the pastor's discipling. But one elementary course is not sufficient qualification. Unfortunately, some pastors are too weak intellectually themselves to grow sturdy saints very effectively. They are strong on arousements but feeble on instruction because they are not deep students. They feel but do not think. As a consequence they are unwitting roadblocks to the growth of their people.

The weakness is compounded by the disposition of some to disparage indoctrination. The famous R. W. Dale of Birmingham, England, was wiser. When he began his pastorate as a young man, the church officers warned him, "These people won't stand for doctrinal preaching." He replied, "They will have to stand for it." They stood it for forty-five years. He understood his calling.

The Scriptures have some trenchant things to say about this. The antichrist will succeed in deluding the religious world because people do not receive "the love of the truth so as to be saved" (2 Thess. 2:10, NASB). Paul commanded Timothy not to permit his elders "to teach false doctrines any longer" (1 Tim. 1:3). Could this today apply to Sunday school teachers? This writer has more than once shuddered at the heretical nonsense propounded in adult classes. It was impossible not to wonder whether the pastor had any awareness of this. Did he have any sense of responsibility or make some kind of an effort to know what was being taught in his Sunday school?

Paul instructs Timothy, "Until I come devote yourself to the public reading of Scripture, to preaching and to teaching" (1 Tim. 4:13). Then Paul adds, "Watch your life and doctrine closely. Persevere in them, because if you do, you will save both yourself and your hearers" (v. 16).

The man whose primary goal is to build a superchurch at any cost will avoid rugged doctrine, especially holiness doctrine. Doctrine declares positions and thus divides people. It always has and always will. The man bitten by the superchurch bug will be tempted to avoid anything that would draw lines, so he will aim at a bland, inoffensive, undemanding, all-things-to-all-people type of ministry. He will operate his church on the philosophy of meeting people's felt needs—forgetting that their felt needs may not be their real needs. But the one who would save souls for eternity will put faithfulness ahead of numbers.

Indoctrination is a bad word only with the superficial and insincere. A pastor's concern for the indoctrination of his people is in direct relation to the depth of his own beliefs. If he is unsure, he is willing for his people to be unsure. If he is tolerant of theological pluralism, he will be comfortable when his people are. If his doctrinal commitment is tepid, he will not lose any sleep over similar mildness in the beliefs of his people.

"Be diligent," Timothy is exhorted, "to present yourself approved to God as a workman who does not need to be ashamed, handling accurately the word of truth" (2 Tim. 2:15, NASB). We are in the day predicted, when many "will not endure sound doctrine, but wanting to have their ears tickled, they will accumulate for themselves teachers in accordance with their own desires" (2 Tim. 4:3, NASB). Some pastors are selling out to accommodate. But a sanctified man will not sell out. He will courageously hold "fast the faithful word which is in accordance with the teaching, that he may be able both to exhort in sound doctrine and to refute those who contradict" (Titus 1:9, NASB). Controversy may have its perils, but its perils are not so deadly as those of pulpit wimpishness. Jude pleads with the church to "contend earnestly for the faith which was once for all delivered to the saints" (Jude 3, NASB). Doctrinal flabbiness enervates the church, undermines its witness, robs its members of religious certainty, and softens church members for the inroads of the cults. Unindoctrinated Christians are without intellectual defenses. Therefore, to fail to indoctrinate is to betray our trust.

THE ART OF INDOCTRINATION

Pastors who feel incapable themselves can begin by saturating their congregations with holiness literature. Book tables should be in every church foyer with clear, sound holiness books on display. While the self-help and self-understanding books, half psychology and half religion, have value, they do not put meat on the bones in the way that deep devotional books do or the expositions of doctrine do.[1] Actually dozens of books, old and new, some simple, some technical, are available and should be circulating continuously in every holiness church. Sometimes classes can be built around some such book as a text, either in the Sunday school or elsewhere.

Even if the pastor is weak in the pulpit, there is still no excuse for doctrinal ignorance if he can persuade his people to read and study, both alone and in groups. However, the pastor has an obligation to learn to articulate doctrine himself, both in sermon and in group situations. Let him follow textbooks if need be. After all, college and seminary professors do, so why shouldn't he?

The art of indoctrination includes ways to inform the mind and then build emotional attachments and strong loyalties to certain doctrines. Some may become overly dogmatic, but in time the Lord will help such persons achieve a balance between firm belief and excessive argumentativeness over details. The important thing is that strong Christians are those who believe some things strongly.

In this process people need to be helped to distinguish between private notions, personal preferences, speculative opinions, and bedrock convictions important enough to die for. People have carried on crusades for years about some emotional prejudice, such as whether Christ was crucified on Friday or Thursday, or some darling prophetic notion, or the exclusive sanctity of the King James Version, only to find in the end that all their verbosity and emotional energy had been expended on a theological dead end.

The pastor who would indoctrinate systematically seeks to give to his people:

A vocabulary;
A conceptual framework;
A biblical base; and
A bridge to life.

In developing the vocabulary the primary tools are the Bible and the creeds. Let the pastor use biblical terms for the various stages of salvation experience and explain those terms. Sanctification is a Bible term—why avoid it? So also are holiness and perfection. Let's not join the chorus of "So Who's Perfect?" and stop there so long as our people will go home and read in the Bible, "Be perfect, therefore, as your heavenly Father is perfect" (Matt. 5:48). If there is a difference between Christian perfection and absolute flawlessness, then say so, with such biblical support and clarity that the people will never again be befuddled over a concept that in holiness circles is at once professed and denied.

The conceptual framework may be summarized as follows:

1. *Theism as a worldview,* distinct from deism, pantheism, or materialism. God is both transcendent and immanent. He is both Creator of the universe and sovereign Governor through law, providence, and judgment.

2. *The eternal triunity of the Godhead,* with the Persons assuming distinct functions in the redemptive plan—the Father as Lawgiver and Initiator, the Son as Revealer and Redeemer, the Spirit as Executive, implementing the processes of redemption. He is God-in-relation.

3. *The inviolability of the divine holiness,* which not only excludes wrongdoing by God but excludes toleration of moral wrong. From this come the necessity of the Atonement and the necessity of eternal retribution against those who reject the Atonement.

4. *The supernatural nature of Christianity,* by which is meant the grounding of Christianity on the redemptive acts of God in ways not explainable or accountable on naturalistic premises. The miracles that constitute Christianity's structure are the Incarnation by means of the Virgin Birth, the bodily resurrection of Christ from the dead, His ascension into heaven as our contemporary Savior and Intercessor; the Pentecost event with all that issues from it, including the church; and the finalized production of the Bible as the Word of God written.

5. *The nature of man as a unique being created in God's image,* male and female, with capacity for moral change, either into Christlike holiness or demonic depravity; a capacity predicated on the power of choice, either to obey God or rebel. That men and women are accountable moral agents destined to answer to their Creator is a basic assumption of Christianity.

6. *The cruciality of sin in the human predicament,* including an inherited bent to sinning due to Adam and Eve's disobedience, and the voluntary commission of known wrong. This concept distinguishes sin from mistakes, infirmities, ignorances, and weaknesses, which are the nonvolitional scars of the Fall. Christianity sees sin (not illness, ignorance, poverty, or political systems) as the supreme impediment to happiness and peace.

7. *The degrading and damning power of sin,* in its debasement of human character, its blighting of human life, and its present and eternal alienation from God.

8. *The moral structure of life,* by which is meant the law of consequences ("we are free to choose but we are not free to choose the consequences of our choices"), and the law of affinity—that the universe is on the side of righteousness and against sin. Sin produces ultimate

pain, righteousness produces ultimate harmony and happiness.

9. *The probationary nature of human life on earth,* with eternal hell the outcome of confirmed unbelief and disobedience and eternal heaven the outcome of sustained faith and obedience.

10. *The necessity of a blood atonement,* offered by Christ in His death on the cross, as God's requirement for the satisfaction of both justice and mercy, and as God's prescribed basis for forgiveness, reconciliation, sanctification, the Spirit's indwelling, and eternal life.

11. *Salvation from sin and the recovery of lost holiness,* including the cleansing of the carnal mind and the full reinhabitation of the Spirit, as the primary objective of Christ's mission, and the central overarching theme of the Bible.

12. *The universality of the Atonement's provisional benefits, and the conditionality of the Atonement's ulitmate personal benefits.* God's saving economy does not include the arbitrary regeneration of the "elect" based on divine decree, with the rest of humanity left without viable options. Neither does the Atonement "lock in" the born-again person to eternal life apart from his ongoing choice to believe and obey.

13. *The grace-system of redemption:* The personal problem of sin cannot be overcome by human initiative but only by responding to God's initiative; furthermore, it cannot be overcome by law-keeping or good works, but only by a humble and penitent acknowledgment of our sinfulness and full acceptance of God's unmerited favor offered in Christ; and the full appropriation of God's grace as an inner power for holiness.

14. *The pivotal place of prevenient grace in the divine economy,* seen as a universal benefit of the Atonement, ministered by the Spirit, which counteracts total

depravity in every human being sufficiently to make all persons salvable, and starts the first flow of desires toward God and salvation.

15. *The radical newness of life in Christ,* which makes impossible the commingling of saving faith and continued willful sinning.

16. *The experiential nature of salvation,* which is individual, personal, and conscious—involving a real "I-Thou" relationship with God (a "know-so" salvation).

17. *The sequence of stages in the Christian life,* involving regeneration and entire sanctification as distinct works of grace, both received by faith in a moment and witnessed to by the Spirit, both preceded and followed by gradual processes of awakening, conviction, learning, and growth.

18. *The obligatory nature of spiritual formation* by which is meant that growth in grace is what Christians are commanded to do (2 Peter 3:18), and that it will not occur as God intends unless deliberate attention is given to the means of grace and to the dynamics of growth.

These are the great conceptual elements of the Christian religion, which pastors are expected to make thoroughly familiar and understandable to their people.[2] These should become the very warp and woof of their thinking, so profoundly internalized that all else in life will be shaped by them.

There are certain especially critical areas, such as the distinction between sins and mistakes, intentions and performance, carnality and normal humanity, temptation and sin. We need to help them understand something of the nature of love as being a godlike commitment to the glory of God and the welfare of others, a love that transcends feelings and that is yielding without being spineless, forgiving without being maudlin, understanding without surrendering one's sense of justice or erasing the boundaries of right and wrong. There is a circle of holy love that sees its source to be in God, mediated through Calvary to our hearts, but flowing back to God and to God's Law *first,* then flowing out to people. Our love for people must be structured by our love for God and His Law—then we will love people as He wants us to love them rather than as we want to love them or as they want us to love them.

All of these distinctions belong to the inculcation of Christian truth essential for living. Only then will our people be rescued from the sentimental rubbish they pick up from this morally bankrupt society.

In building a vocabulary and conceptual framework no better tool is at hand, next to the Bible, than the creeds. A series of sermons on the doctrinal statements of one's denomination would be useful periodically. It would serve two purposes—sharpen and realign the pastor's own thinking, and educate the church.

Church music is also a supportive tool. John and Charles Wesley knew the power of a sound hymnody. What people sing in church they probably sing at home. What they sing at home seeps into their subconscious and enriches the treasury of their doctrinal attachments. If a pastor's minister of music keeps the people jigging to empty ditties, he should fire the musician and find one with a better understanding of his mission.[3]

But further than this we cannot go in this book. Pastors who believe this understanding of salvation and who experience its reality in their own lives, will find a way to learn to handle the doctrine effectively and convincingly. But their preaching must be rich in texture. All facets of this diamond need to be held up to the light. And the preaching must be so precise that the listeners are not left in a fog. What they hear must be understood by them as the preaching of regeneration and entire sanctification as two distinct works of grace. This will be the point of offense, and this will be the criterion of faithfulness.[4]

Perhaps the real test of whether or not so-called holiness preaching is authentically biblical and Wesleyan is a very simple one: Is the preaching helping anyone find "the blessing"? Are believers receiving light on the subject, and reflectively receiving light on their own need, and becoming so hungry that they become seekers and then finders? Are there folk around who can testify to a clear experience of entire sanctification who could not so testify before we came? And are they testifying?

For this to be true, holiness preaching, in one or other of its facets, must mark a pastor's year-round ministry, not be an occasional shock treatment. For, in the words of D. G. Kehle, "one learns doctrine through repetition, whether the doctrine be commercial, satanic, or divine."[5]

14

SOME CRUCIAL AREAS
OF NURTURE

S ome areas of nurture are more difficult than others,
requiring unusual thought and labor on the part of
the pastor. For this reason pastors may allow certain
emphases to drop through the cracks. But when this
occurs the maturing process of new converts and the
church as a whole is short-circuited.

THE CHRISTIANIZING OF VALUES

While indoctrination is the foundation of healthful
growth and spiritual stability, it must include more than a
head knowledge of the essential tenets of the Christian
religion. It must be the indoctrination of the heart as well.
Built into the Christian should be not only intellectual
understandings and underpinnings but personal habits and
lifestyles that become the practice of the truth.

Consciously or unconsciously everyone is controlled
by his value system. Some things receive prior attention,
energy, and time because in his value system they are of
prime importance. Other values range down the ladder,
and can be more willingly pushed aside. The worldly

mind is shaped in its value system by the sales pitch of the world. The body is at the top of the list, hence exercise is more important than church. Some think loyalty to their bowling team the most important. Others wouldn't think of missing the Wednesday night square dance. These are samples of the world's value systems, and they illustrate how such systems dictate choices.

Our new converts bring into the Christian life with them at least a residue of their habitual and respective value systems. Reshaping them will be the first big hurdle in learning how to live the Christian life. Regeneration radically recasts one's perspective, so that now spiritual claims are seen as First Claims. God has been brought into the center. But a lot of previous baggage is dragged in also, on the assumption that because these things are not essentially sinful they can be continued as part of life. So sports, travel, accumulation of the latest gadgets, TV favorites, bowling night, boats and boating, et cetera, continue to fill up life as before.

But the new Christian quickly begins to discover that these old activities are competing with his new commitments. Gradually it dawns on him that if he is going to attend prayer meeting, Wednesday bowling must go. Rapidly with some, but with others slowly, the whole lifestyle will undergo a radical overhaul—compelled by the inner change in perspective by which comparative values are determined. At some point along the line, the cleansing crisis of entire sanctification will be crucial to this process.

This process belongs to that essential "renewing" of the mind (Rom. 12:2). It is learning to think like a Christian. A Christian who thinks like a Christian sees that holiness is more important than happiness, heaven more important than earth, eternity more important than time, and God more important than people. Fun and frolic, fads and fashions, VCRs and cameras, hobbies and clubs, begin to be seen as less and less important, and gradually are submerged by more urgent activities, activities that are now perceived to be of *eternal consequence*. Unless this process of revamping one's value system goes forward to its Christian conclusion, spiritual growth will be stymied and backsliding will set in. To repeat: the deeper internal spiritualization of one's nature by entire sanctification will be the crucial factor in aiding one through this reorganizing period.

DEEPENING THE GODWARD RELATIONSHIP

Doctrine without devotion will produce a well-mapped desert. Pastors are wise to speak frequently of the importance of prayer. Stress should be on the intimate love relationship between the believer and God, which marks the normal Christian life. Prayer is keeping in constant touch with Christ our Friend. It must not be seen as a burden but as a privilege, as delightful as visiting with earthly friends we love.

It is to be expected that the new Christian will have some problems at first. He may struggle with feelings of unreality, for when he talks with spouse or children or neighbor he can *see* them. They are obviously real. But where is God? Prayer to some seems like talking into empty space. But here too doctrine guides the mind in its understanding of the Triune God, who not only created and rules and not only walked as a man in Galilee and Judea but who as the Holy Spirit is present with us each moment. If we acknowledge His presence, He will make Himself real to us. Hebrews 11:6 is appropriate here: "Without faith it is impossible to please God, because anyone who comes to him must believe that he exists and that he rewards those who earnestly seek him."

Then the problems of wandering thoughts and restlessness will plague. Most difficult to solve is the problem of finding time to get alone with God. This will be difficult for everyone—women, men, young people. But the pastor must help them see that God is the most important Person in their lives, and time spent with Him is the most important appointment that they can ever keep. Talking to God is grander, nobler, more pregnant with potential for life than any possible conversation with kings or presidents. To say these things is not to be rhetorical. It is simply to acknowledge the truth. Can we help new Christians see and feel this? If so, they will not groan about having to find time to pray, but will delight in the challenge of solving their personal dilemmas. Eagerness will spark ingenuity, and they will find all sorts of ways for adjusting this and dispensing with that in order to have a solid block of time alone with their Lord.

That sacred period of time should include quiet, unhurried reading of the Word; also meditation, praise, petition, and intercession. But always the Christian needs to think of it as an intimate conversation with an unseen but very real and close and understanding Friend. And he should feel free to express himself fully—his doubts, complaints, longings, defeats. Everything that comprises his life, whether domestic or social or vocational, is a fit subject of prayer. Christians should be encouraged to believe that nothing is too small for them to bring to God. If it is important enough to talk about, it is important enough to pray about.

All tampering with occult meditation systems must be avoided. Trying to meditate with the aid of a *mantra,* for instance, is an insult to the Holy Spirit.

In the early days of one's Christian life frequent

recommitments to a prayer regimen may be necessary, as the pressures of life will tend to bend our plans and intrude into the secret closet. But no matter how many times a growing Christian may have to reassess his schedule and reestablish his prayer commitment, he must understand that this is to be rigorously done; for it is as basic to life and health as are meals and sleep.

The pastor can also help new Christians understand that while spiritual appetites are a gift of grace in one sense, yet they are also to be cultivated. A deep love for prayer, a sense of ease on one's knees, a spirit of prayer through the day, a real love for the Bible are all marks of Christian maturity, and will be the end product of faithfulness during the days we struggle with disinterest and sluggishness and unreality. Acquiring a real delight in the Scripture and in communion with our heavenly Father is part of the learning and growing process.

If a pastor is going to succeed in nurturing the prayer life of his people, he must see to it that his total church life is structured by an emphasis on prayer meetings. The pastor must make every effort to draw new converts into women's, men's, youth, mid-week, and home prayer meetings. They should be encouraged, without undue pressure, to take part.

Elementary sentence prayer sessions will be the easiest ice-breaker. However, the church is itself immature if sentence praying is all its members are capable of doing. In every church there should be a corps of prayer warriors who know how to call on God and engage in protracted prevailing prayer. New converts should find themselves also in this kind of a prayer situation. Even though they only listen and wonder, their growth will accelerate, and they will imbibe a *standard* which will immunize them against the perpetuation of infantile piety.

LEARNING THE JOYS OF STEWARDSHIP

Responsible handling of their resources is also an area of discipling (as introduced in chapter twelve). Very soon a new Christian should be taught the duty and privilege of tithing. Sermons, tracts, classes, testimonies of others will all play a part in helping the neophyte see that this is just part of serving God. A nontither is still an outsider. He is a guest in the house. Tithing makes one an insider. One is now part of the team, sharing with others gladly and unselfishly the responsibility of keeping the doors open and spreading the gospel.

Tithing is an act of faith. The very idea of taking ten percent and giving it to the church is at first shocking and often precipitates a deep struggle. "How can we do it?" Not knowing the wonderful ways of God, the new Christian may regard the practice as impossible for him, even unethical in the face of current obligations and debts. Let the pastor put into timid hands some such book as *Your Money Matters* by Malcolm MacGreggor, and perhaps their faith will become strong enough to plunge into the practice of tithing, fearfully but courageously, as an act of obedience.

Three aspects of this will require careful, repetitive instruction. One is that we do not tithe in order to be prospered. Tithing is part of our service. It is an act of devotion. Second, tithing is indispensable to spiritual growth. It is part of living the Christian life. People who fear or refuse to tithe never prosper spiritually.

But the third aspect is that tithing is but the acknowledgement of our total stewardship. Christians should learn to think in terms of God's ownership of themselves and all they have or hope to have. As stewards their aim in life is to extend the kingdom of the Lord Jesus Christ. All of life is consecrated and disciplined to contribute to this supreme end, and anything that cannot contribute is willingly surrendered. The Christian lives for God and souls. His private happiness is under tribute to this Christian perspective. Therefore, the tithe is a token of the whole. Financial support of the Lord's work begins with the tithe, but does not end with it. Gradually the joy of giving will be learned, until the Christian will delight in giving more and more of his resources.

But far beyond money, he himself will be at the Lord's disposal. Talents, time, energies, and possessions as well as vocation and avocation will all be seen by the believer as belonging to God. Stewardship will come to be seen not simply as a passive availability, languidly acknowledged, but as an aggressive, intense application of all one's powers. This is the way the wholly sanctified believer feels and thinks. This is a fundamental facet of heart holiness. Stewardship and holiness can almost be said to be two names for the same thing.

HOME RELIGION

All Christians must learn to put God's plumbline on their human relations. For many the chief arena of struggle will be the home. If they are to become sturdy saints they must learn to be saintly there. Yet many of them struggle with their more intimate interpersonal relationships: with unsaved spouses, parents with unruly children and associated disciplinary challenges, and with burdens of livelihood and money/property management. It is one thing to be converted, another to be cleansed of the carnal mind, but yet another to learn to cope with the nuts and bolts of everyday living. And the most ideal school for the developing of sainthood is the home.

Pastors will need to give much attention to the home challenge through their counseling, their pastoral calling, and in such auxiliary ministries as Marriage Enrichment Retreats. In most instances the two bottlenecks are lack of wisdom and lack of understanding. If somehow young husbands can be helped to understand their wives and live with them according to 1 Peter 3:7, domestic tranquillity and happiness will in many cases finally move in. And if young wives can learn to understand their husbands and see with loving discernment their hurts and fears and needs, they themselves will be more relaxed and happier. But this paragraph merely serves to remind the pastor of one facet of his job, if he is to grow sturdy saints.

RELATING TO THE WORLD AROUND

New converts have been brought out of the world into the church. They have correctly seen the necessity of separation and abstention, according to 2 Corinthians 6:14–7:1. But they cannot hibernate within the four walls of a church building. They must go back out into the world to acquire an education, do business, make a living, contribute to society. They will be rubbing elbows with the unsaved every day, even at home in many cases, certainly on the job.

Can the pastor help these Christians find the balance between being *in* the world but not *of* it? A sound independence of peers, of trends and fads, and a discernment of what is proper and what is improper, what is legitimate for a Christian and what is not are all marks of Christian depth and stability.

Certain emphases are vital. One is the art of witnessing with wisdom. If a Christian is weak, withdrawal is the way of wisdom. But if he feels himself to be strong enough to mingle socially to some degree, he should be motivated always by soul-winning concerns. This should be aggressive, uppermost in one's thinking and planning, and supported by much prayer. Social contacts should not be times for hiding one's light but for seeking ways and means of witnessing.

Unfortunately, many young Christians tend to be hopelessly naïve. They are lambs in the midst of experienced and designing wolves. For the first few years of their Christian life, they had better stick as much as possible to their own crowd, and not branch out except as their occupations demand intermingling; and unless and until they have had some training and are themselves definitely led by the Spirit, perhaps they should team up with another Christian.

TEACHING CHRISTIAN ETHICS

Another important pastoral tutorial emphasis must be on basic Christian ethics. This is a demanding area of ministry, requiring careful thought, thorough study, and prayerful courage. Christians need to understand that (in the words of R. Duane Thompson), "Communion with God is not simply an end in itself; social and ethical righteousness, with power to transform the social setting, is a natural and necessary component."[1]

The general principle is that the pastor needs to remind people continually of the basic requirements of righteousness. The Ten Commandments should be expounded periodically, together with the plethora of supporting and expanding passages in the New Testament. Chief of these would be the Sermon on the Mount, then Romans 12–14, Galatians 5, Ephesians 4–6, and many others.

Christians should never be permitted to forget that they are to practice secretly and publicly unimpeachable honesty and purity. New converts often bring into the Christian life years of confused ethical thinking and shady practices. It takes time and instruction for their sense of right and wrong to get straightened out. A good conscience (1 Tim. 1:5) is not only clear through forgiveness but educated by the Bible. Expounding biblical ethics belongs to the pastor's discipling task.

Then the field of ethics includes also those special positions taken by most holiness churches. They are called Church Rules. These should not be seen as roadblocks to freedom but preservations of freedom. They should not be seen as tolerated nuisances but as badges of courage and honor. They are not barriers behind which we cower but standards by which we march. To put it differently—the pastor is not sufficiently competent if the church rules continue to be seen as excess baggage and are an embarrassment to him. Christians are not yet thinking straight unless they are so committed to everything that is right and so opposed to everything that is wrong that they will daily thank God for a church that dares to take open, unabashed stands on moral and ethical issues.

Preaching once a year on the rules of one's denomination, as a duty, is self-defeating. Nothing will more surely create scorn both for the preacher and the rules. If the rules are not germane to present discipleship every day, and if they are not relevant to the tides of life reflected daily in the newspaper, then they are vestigial tabus of the past. Instead of dusting them off and displaying them nostalgically once a year they should be forgotten. But if the rules represent biblical principles and ethical positions vital to the spiritual and moral welfare of contemporary Christians, they should be handled with the respect and competence they deserve.

Fundamental to that competence is pastoral fire. If a pastor truly loves people, he will be intensely interested in trends and practices that affect his people and society in general. In every faithful pastor is the soul of the prophet.

He will be capable of holy warfare. There will be in him the ardent heart of a crusader. Therefore, he will blend into his total preaching program frequent forays into ethical territory, with force and conviction. The result will be an ethically informed and responsive people.

The pastor will need to make special effort to reestablish certain basic moral convictions in the minds of people in his congregation who have suffered the brainwashing of the media and whose convictions have been eroded. These include legal public gambling, sex outside of marriage, living together without marriage, easy divorce, the use of alcohol, and casual abortion. Every Sunday the pastor is facing some folk who have become mushy and loose in their thinking about such issues. But meeting the needs of these people will require more than tirades. It will call for careful biblical exposition and thoroughly competent ethical reasoning. But no mincing.[2]

It is fundamental to Christian ethics that we learn to live by principle. This will go beyond the letter of the law and involve applying the inner principle of the letter to situations not named precisely. Such skill in applying principles will give Christians a moral discernment in their TV viewing, in their places of recreation and entertainment, and in business and social complexities. The legalist will run to the church discipline to see if this or that is named. If it is not named, he will feel free to indulge. The mature ethicist will ask if the moral *principle* underlying the rule is being violated. The goal of Christian growth is the maturity that sifts life daily along these lines spontaneously and naturally because the conscience is trained to discern what is compatible with holiness and what is not. "Solid food is for the mature, who by constant use have trained themselves to distinguish good from evil" (Heb. 5:14).

Another basic principle is that acceptability in the Christian life of a particular practice is determined by its potential impact on others. Here Romans 14–15 is a treasure store of instruction.

Yet another principle which must be inculcated is that activities are ethically evaluated not just in terms of obvious hurtfulness at the moment but in terms of intrinsic trends and ultimate directions. The Puritan Thomas Greenham taught that not only is sin forbidden but its occasion as well, i.e., anything which tends to lead to sin. This of course is the rationale behind opposition to the social dance, the use of regular playing cards, and many questionable practices. In teaching these truths, the pastor could well make frequent use of Susanna Wesley's wise counsel: "Whatever weakens your reason, impairs the tenderness of your conscience, obscures your sense of God, or takes off the relish of spiritual things, whatever increases the authority of your body over mind, that thing for you is sin."

This leads to a yet further principle which belongs to the pastor's pedagogical task. It is essential that people see that avoidance of this or that should not be out of fear or duty but out of love for God. Their affections should be profoundly conditioned to "abhor that which is evil and cleave to that which is good" (Rom. 12:9, KJV). Then avoidance will not seem like a deprivation for which they feel slightly sorry for themselves. Neither will the rules seem like an infringement on their liberties. If their moral sense is sound, they will hate what God hates, with instant recoil and internalized rejection. For such people the printed rule will be useful for guidance and instruction but needless for motivation.

15

PASTORAL COUNSELING: ITS UNIQUENESS

I was once about to enter a church to address a group of pastors, and at the last moment I whimsically turned to a couple of solid laymen and asked, "What shall I say to them?" Like a flash they answered, "Talk to them about preaching, organizing, and counseling." Obviously counseling was high on the agenda of their concerns.

How would these two laymen have defined counseling? Since I do not know, I will attempt a definition without their help. Counseling is the act of verbally helping another person find the proper solution to a particular problem. The problem may be conceptual: intellectual help is wanted. It may be dispositional: how can I change? It may be situational: what should I do?

Counseling involves listening to the recital of the problem, mutually exploring and uncovering its facets, exploring possible answers, and ultimately settling on an answer. The answer may involve a change of attitude or a course of action or both. In a sense the solution is arrived at mutually. Yet if helpful change is to occur, the solution must be the counselee's. It will not be enough for him to submit to the counselor's solution, no matter how wise and correct it may be. Sooner or later the counselee must embrace it and in every sense make it his own. He must be able to say to himself, "I see what I must do."

Totally avoiding counseling is virtually impossible for any pastor who takes his calling seriously and has in any measure a shepherd's heart. People are problem-prone. These are days of incredible complexities and confusions. The daily media bombard the minds of our people with clashing ideals and brazen challenges to everything held dear. Centuries-old traditions and standards are mangled everywhere. The licentious and lawless mood of the day seeps into our homes, creating rebellion in the children and tension between spouses. The two or three cars which take family members in different directions every day, the several TVs blaring at night in different parts of the house, the frenetic pace to keep up with too many activities, including the activities of the church, keep our people at nerve's end. They live too near the snapping point. Out of this modern social cauldron suicides multiply at all age levels. Mental illness has become almost epidemic. Our technological knowledge explosion leaves people confused and depressed because they feel helpless, unable to keep up. The age has outstripped the coping ability of many. For relief they turn to drugs, sex, excitement, affairs. Even Christians are not unscathed. These are the people who listen hungrily to the pastor's sermon, and who welcome him into their homes, or appear at his study door, reaching desperately for a stabilizing and guiding word.

KINDS OF PROBLEMS

Most problems fall into the following categories:

1. *Spiritual.* These people are uncertain about their spiritual state. They may be struggling with temptations

and/or guilt feelings. They are troubled about their reactions, and trying to sort them out in relation to heart holiness. They may be beset with doubts, even unbelief. They are deeply puzzled by the mysteries of Providence. The enigmas of accidents, natural evils, and death challenge their faith. The Bible raises questions in their minds. They desire a deeper understanding of the Bible and of the basic tenets of their faith. Or they may have trouble praying. God seems not to answer. Perhaps they have discovered their doublemindedness and feel a growing hunger for the fullness of the Spirit. But questions plague them about this experience which they need to talk out.

2. *Moral*. These people may be struggling with some overwhelming temptation. Perhaps they have already sinned, and find themselves caught in a home-wrecking trap. Or they have been defeated by old habits. At the office or in an ungodly home, they feel that they are almost to be swept off their feet by the powerful undertow of worldliness and fleshliness. Or they may be facing ethical decisions at work, respecting "tricks of the trade" expected of them. Or students have cheated and now don't know what to do about it. Perhaps the ethical questions with which they are wrestling may be the vexing issue of church rules; or, more broadly, the permissiveness of the day respecting sex before marriage, living together unmarried, abortion; or in another area, civil disobedience or struggles about such things as military registration. About all these painful issues the plausible arguments swirling around them may have made the lines of right and wrong less clear-cut. Of course such ethical problems are spiritual also but in a special category of their own.

3. *Domestic*. This is the most common type of problem which brings church members to the pastor's study (or prompts them to phone or ask for a home call,

or which sends them to a public altar hoping for help there). And in this category spouse trouble dominates. Most of these flaps are practical and emotional, but they may be in the moral category also. Experienced pastors are no longer shocked to discover that some of their "first" families are not free from internal stress. It may range all the way from incompatibility to physical abuse. It may cover mental cruelty, "kinky" sex, sex deprivation, illicit infatuations. At worst, actual adultery. In some cases, even incest. Or husband and wife may simply seem to be drifting apart, and do not know how to rekindle the flame of their love and reaffirm their basic commitment.

A close second to spouse trouble is the hurt and perplexity of having *lost control over children*. Perhaps drug use has been discovered, or teen-age sexual activity, even pregnancy. Or it may be generalized rebellion, with adoption of unwholesome peer standards, combined with defiance and disrespect. These are crushing experiences for Christian parents who thought they were doing well and who had hoped for better things. When the children were small they glibly, even smugly, quoted Proverbs 22:6, "Train up a child in the way he should go: and when he is old, he will not depart from it" (KJV). They are silent now, filled with guilt and grief. They need a wise shepherd.

Or the domestic problem may be *financial*. Authorities say that money is the number-one cause of quarrels and separations. I am inclined to think that in many cases money disagreements are only symptoms of deeper rifts. However, at times money really is the primary issue. But the culprit is not money but diverse and even opposite approaches to money. A husband who is a tightwad and secretive; who always has money for what he wants but never for what his wife wants; or who keeps the family up to its neck in debt—such husbands are a menace to home happiness, for they drive wedges, breed resentment and bitterness, incite perpetual bickering, and create a generally oppressive atmosphere.

But the shoe fits the other foot equally well. In many households it is the wife who is the compulsive, undisciplined spender and who keeps her husband in financial hot water. Or she is a nagger about money, always needling him because he doesn't make more, and provide for her more affluently.

The potential for trouble in the money sector of family life is limitless. Where does pastoral counseling come into this picture? Normally, not at all until strains have reached the explosion point. Then the pastor will be fortunate if they come to him first rather than to a lawyer.

4. *Interpersonal.* Trouble with other persons is a prime category of problems that will consume a pastor's time in counseling. People have a great facility for drifting into painful dislocations and strains in their human relationships. Many times the origin is not evil intent but immaturity, misunderstanding, supersensitivity, lack of tact, even forgetfulness. The rupture may be with neighbors, relatives (especially in-laws), or fellow-workers on the job. Or the break may be with fellow Christians in the church. People will be hurt by others and come to the pastor with their hurts. Or they may be ashamed of their own role and come for counsel concerning possible solutions.

5. *Physical.* Health problems normally take people to medical doctors but often to their pastor too, many times first. They hope for healing and want anointing and prayer. Or they may need counsel concerning how to relate their illness to the will of God and the promises of the Bible. Or even respecting the choice of physicians— though this is more uncommon.

When life is too crowded and hectic, the body sooner

or later will rebel in some form of illness. These people need help in slowing their pace, rediscovering their priorities, and taking the surplus irons out of the fire. Fatigue not only breeds physical illness but is a prime cause of interpersonal ruptures and spiritual confusion.

6. *Emotional.* This is a catch-all category, as problems in any of the above areas will affect the emotions. The peril is always that the emotional upset may become a greater problem than the problem which occasioned it. If emotions get out of hand and become disabling so that normal, mature coping is prevented, the result may be what Australians call a "cot case." Depression, hysteria, panic, anxiety, fear are all debilitating emotions that may arise out of stressful situations, even those which in themselves could be surmounted by good management and common sense. When persons give in to runaway emotions they only compound their problems.

With a carnal person, the matter is even more aggravated, for the emotions may include temper tantrums, pouting, orgies of self-pity, resentment and bitterness, perhaps a retaliatory spirit, or even ugly, unrestrained outbursts of verbal venom.

Happy is the pastor whose people come to him with their problems when they are relatively fluid, and the persons involved are still open to reason. In the development of a problem, a point is reached when attitudes, forged in the heat of intemperate emotion, become less amenable—soon not amenable at all—to calm counseling and rational thinking. At this stage the attempt by the pastor to bring sanity back into the situation requires great wisdom. In fact, the poison may have progressed so far that people will turn on the pastor instead of submitting to him. It is sad when persons, perhaps a family, will monopolize a pastor's time and energy for weeks, then in the end become his worst enemies.

There are other various serious emotional problems, many of which are beyond the average pastor's expertise. But he should know how to recognize them and when and to whom to refer them. An example is *post-traumatic stress disorder,* which is a prolonged syndrome of reaction to extreme trauma, such as war, civilian catastrophe (e.g., plane crash), or natural disaster (such as a tornado). Such emotional upheavals may be deep, complex, and persistent. The pastor can stand by and give unfailing support, but he may also need the aid of Christian psychiatrists or psychologists.

KEEPING COUNSELING PASTORAL

No facet of a pastor's ministry is more delicate and downright dangerous than counseling. It is the occasion of a pastor's undoing perhaps more often than any other form of ministerial activity. Yet it does not need to be one's Waterloo, if one will simply bring to this service some reasonable degree of common sense. Usually, when things have gone awry, common sense has been lacking. Every pastor should place a prayer on his desk: "Lord, help me to be like Zechariah—a 'wise counselor'" (1 Chron. 26:14).

The underlying principle in pastoral counseling is the necessity of making sure that the counseling is Christian. This requires certain corollaries.

1. *First is the necessity of divine love.* This is more than humanitarian interest in people, which secular professionals might have. It is a grace-generated love that feels for and with the total person, in full awareness of the eternal as well as temporal dimensions. This love is compassionate, patient, perceptive, and gentle, without being maudlin. This is the most essential ingredient in successful counseling—not Solomonic wisdom or great

learning. For in many instances the most effective thing a pastor can do is listen with understanding, offer a prayer, and give an encouraging word. The troubled person goes away helped. He or she has new courage to face the impossible situation.

2. *A wise pastoral counselor never forgets the nature of his calling.* At this point, it is necessary to say that common sense needs the foundation of a sound philosophy. Earlier an attempt was made to define counseling. But does the addition of "pastoral" make any significant difference? Yes, a radical difference, for the controlling term is not "counseling" but "pastoral." Here is not a counselor who happens to be a pastor; rather, here is a pastor who happens to be counseling and whose counseling will be authentic only if it is done in fidelity to the primacy of the pastoral role.

This defines the pastor's role before God and also defines his role with his people. Before God he is called to represent God in Christ, in total fidelity to all the implications of the gospel. His guidelines therefore are not to be found in secular psychology but in the Holy Scriptures. His viewpoint is thoroughly religious. His objective is to bring men and women to God, direct them in the path of holiness, and seek by all means to shepherd them all the way to heaven. Their salvation is his uppermost objective, always; their happiness, health, prosperity, and mental soundness are only secondarily his objectives. These are humanitarian interests about which he feels profoundly—probably much more deeply than those who talk most about them—but his involvement in these earthly matters must never become such a preoccupation that he forgets the primary consideration: their relationship with God. Other practitioners can treat people as patients or clients; the pastor must see them as never-dying souls.

In his searching critique of modern Protestant trends in pastoral care, Don S. Browning observes that too many pastors "are aspiring to fashion their ministry more and more according to the model of the secular psychotherapist."[1] They "are envying and imitating a bit too much the tidy focus and apparent expertise of the secular counselor and psychotherapist."[2] In doing so they sacrifice what is most germane to their special calling. He says that the uniquely religious viewpoint of the pastor "should be clear and obvious both to the general public and to the people who come for help in times of need."[3]

Dutch theologian Jacob Firet states the matter in even more radical terms. The most essential element in pastoral role-fulfillment, including the role of counselor, he declares, is in the fact that here is a person "who acts, not on his own, not by virtue of his own superiority . . . but in the name of the Lord of the church, and with the word of God." It lies, he says, in the fact that the pastor is being "sent by a specific mandate of the Lord, who wishes to 'make an appearance' himself in the role-fulfillment of the pastor, by means of the word of his revelation laid on and entrusted to him."[4]

This is a staggering conception. But its validity lies, in part at least, in the fidelity with which the pastor knows the Word of God and allows himself to be its authentic voice.

Wise pastors therefore, who know their calling, are well aware of the incongruity of relying on the concepts and tools of secular therapies. The objective in secular counseling is adjustment with the environment: people, situations, self. The desired adjustment is that which will bring optimum peace and normalcy in life's relations. Methods stress acceptance and non-judgmentalism on the part of the counselor and self-acceptance on the part of the counselee. The only behavioral or emotional modification deemed essential is that which seems necessary for the achievement of social homeostasis. The counselor resorts therefore to "eductive counseling" in which solutions are sought within the framework of the counselee's own insights and viewpoints. No attempt is made to influence these mores or viewpoints in a direction more in harmony with the counselor's personal beliefs.

But as Browning points out, while such a neutral, open, accepting approach has much to commend it, "its overemphasis signals a default on the part of the Protestant community."[5] That default is nothing less than shameful betrayal of the Christian faith. For the premise of the Christian counselor is that every person's primary need is not adjustment to his environment but adjustment to God. Since the secular psychologist or therapist will not operate on such a premise, the Christian pastor had better! With him this is the true focus of all of life. If this is not clear, there cannot possibly be ultimate solutions at any other level or in any other category.

Such a sobering awareness of the uniqueness of the pastor's role and mission, which sets him apart from all other counselors, prompts one pastor, who is much in demand, to draw the lines in his first interview. He says, "I am interested in you and your situation. I want to help you if I can. But I must tell you in advance that I will talk to you about God and the salvation of your soul. If you do not want religion, you should go elsewhere."

This is a strong, even radical approach; but it has not driven many away. He still has more counseling than he can comfortably handle. A few go elsewhere, thus saving the pastor much time and heartache. Most accept his help on his terms and respect his stand. The chances of being able to help them meaningfully and lastingly are multiplied many times if the relationship is on such an unequivocal basis right from the start.

3. *A third corollary is the radical difference between the pastor's role as a counselor and the role of the nonpastoral counselor (whether secular or Christian).* The pastor may counsel, but he is not a professional counselor. This is true even if he is well trained and certified. *The relationship of a pastor to a church is a different kind of relationship than that of a professional counselor with his clientele.* Woe be to the person who tries to ignore or break down the essential wall between these two kinds of relationships.

In addition to the radical difference inherent in the nature of the pastor's calling, there are profound psychological and sociological differences. A professional counselor has an office, a program of appointments, specific fees, and often adjacent colleagues. His contact with his client is normally limited to the counseling session. He is a true professional. As such, like a physician, he can query, probe, pursue areas that ought to be out of bounds to a pastor. Why? Because the professional does not relate to his patient or client socially but professionally. The pastor relates to his people socially, all the time. He is their shepherd, their confidant, their friend and brother, their teacher, exhorter, if need be their rebuker, not professionally but fraternally and with true identification, as a sinner saved by grace and as a shepherd with his sheep. Then on Sunday this one who listened to their woes during the week stands up to preach. Those who confided in him during the week should be able to look up to him as God's prophet and God's voice—without too much intimacy.

The bond between this counselee and this Sunday morning preacher is extremely delicate. If in that counseling session he has attempted to be anything other than a pastor leading to God, it will be hard for the counselee on Sunday morning to think of himself as a worshiper and learner. Remembering the counseling session, there may be feelings of embarrassment, uneasiness, distrust, or, worse, cozy attachment, as being someone especially important to this person in the pulpit. All of which injures the relationship both ways: to the pastor as a *counselor* and to the pastor as a *person of God.*

Therefore, it is important that a pastor never think of himself as a professional counselor, or allow himself to be perceived as such by others. He is first and always a pastor, and any counseling he does must be adjunct to that. Not only adjunct but compatible.

4. *A fourth corollary is the necessity of the pastor being thoroughly conversant with Christian theology,* including anthropology, hamartiology, and soteriology. This should include (to repeat) a familiarity with the Bible that enables him to wear it "like a glove" as P. T. Forsyth said. He should understand sin, and know how to distinguish sin from infirmity. This competence in theology can be enriched by supplementary studies in modern psychology, especially by such works as *General Psychology for Christian Counselors* by Ronald L. Koteskey (Abingdon, 1983). The writings of Paul Tournier and more recently the books and films of James Dobson are extremely valuable. But familiarity with and even expertise in contemporary therapies will not compensate for biblical and theological neophytism.

A pastor should have a sound understanding of human nature. This will include a full recognition of its complexity. On the one hand endemic to human nature is aspiration. There is desire for improvement, for betterment, for answers, for solutions. It is aspiration which brings people to the pastor's office. Moreover, people have a conscience, quickened by the Spirit as a boon of prevenient grace. The conscience is the pastor's surest ally. But on the debit side of the ledger is the incredible complexity of motives. Rationalizations and other defense mechanisms stick out all over the place, generally completely hidden from the counselee.

But above all, the pastor needs a realistic understanding of the profound deceptiveness of the human heart. Deep within are lies, lusts, covetousness, hatred, selfishness, cupidity, pride, rebellion against God. These bents and sins of the spirit color one's view of one's problems inevitably and inescapably. There are blind spots and prejudices, combined with stubbornness and trickiness. Let not the pastor be sirened into a rosy optimism by the prevailing pelagianism all around him. The realities of human nature are grim—every bit as evil as the Bible says they are. This helps the pastor avoid naïveté, and thus be more like his Lord, who refused to commit himself prematurely to professed believers, "for he knew what was in man" (John 2:25).

Notwithstanding the complexities of human nature, while the biblically informed pastor will not be easily taken in by a shallow optimism, he will operate on a grander optimism than any counselor around, for he knows not only the depths of sin but the magnificence of the cure. And no one knows this better than a Wesleyan minister. He rejoices in the possibilities of saving and sanctifying grace, which not only can transform the counselee as a person but revolutionize his attitudes and insights into his problems. He knows that a problem not solved along spiritual lines is not solved at all—only whitewashed. But he also knows that Christ can get into seemingly impossible situations and bring about radical and permanent changes, either in the situation or in the counselee, or both. Therefore his pastoral counseling will seek to build faith, and include large amounts of prayer and Bible application.

16

PASTORAL COUNSELING: ITS PERILS

I once read the story of a medical doctor who had gained a reputation as a skillful surgeon. But over the years he became cocky. One morning while making his hospital rounds he picked up the chart of a patient on whom he had performed major surgery a couple days before. The nurse watched him with anxiety, for she knew that warning signs were all over the chart. But the doctor just gave it a quick glance, his thumb all the while over the item most ominous. The nurse knew he would not brook any interference from her and kept still. The patient died. The doctor was too sure of himself.

There are pastors who are too sure of themselves. Those most apt to be so are the very young, and the middle-aged persons who "have it made". But whether young, mature, or in between, no pastor can afford to skip this chapter. The one most apt to skip it, scorning its title, is probably the very one who can least afford to do so. Grave perils lurk everywhere in pastoral counseling, of which every pastor should be humbly and keenly aware.

COUNSELING BEYOND ONE'S EXPERTISE

A wise pastoral counselor will not attempt to counsel beyond his expertise. In the previous chapter it was said that one should not ignore the special bounds of his calling, even if his expertise exceeds that of most ministers. How very important it is, then, for him not to presume expertise that he does not have. We live in a day when ministers as well as doctors may be subject to malpractice suits. Furthermore, there are secular practitioners everywhere who would like nothing better than to see a preacher indicted—or at least exposed and ridiculed—for a kind of counseling for which he was not certified.

Therefore, the responsible pastor will not only know the bounds of his professional calling, but be aware of the peril of exceeding those bounds. He will instead become well acquainted with the various persons and support groups in his community to whom or to which he can refer people who come to him with special, critical needs, even his own members. It will be a kindness to them. There are profound sexual problems, emotional complexes and phobias, mental aberrations and psychoses that require the expert assistance of a specialist. Since so many personal problems are in the area of mental health, a pastor should maintain team relationships with professionals in that field rather than attempting to function as a lone-wolf therapist. The pastor who utilizes these agencies will gain the respect of his community and protect himself from embarrassing entanglements.

THE EQUAL PERIL OF
REFERRING TOO SOON

Yet Martin Bobgan, in *Psychoheresy,* warns us against abdicating our role as Christian ministers by a policy of referral which in effect brings the basic claims of our faith into question.[1] When God assured Paul, "My grace is sufficient for you, for my power is made perfect in weakness" (2 Cor. 12:9), He was proclaiming one of those claims. It seems to have concerned a physical malady that Dr. Luke apparently could not cure and God chose not to, but which involved embarrassment and emotional stress. Paul accepted God's grace as sufficient, and let it go at that; undoubtedly he found that God's grace really was enough. It was a spiritual victory far greater than a simple miracle of healing. We must be careful not to deprive our counselees of such higher solutions.

Many of the problems brought to a pastor are at root spiritual, even though they have physical effects and complications. Experience shows that in many of these cases when the spiritual problem is faced and solved God's way, the physical side effects disappear. Therefore, let us help our counselees to believe in God's grace. Counseling skill consists in helping them lay hold of it. We may abort this kind of spiritual victory by washing our hands of them too soon.

I know of a pastor worked exhaustingly with a heroin addict for three years, many times severely tempted to feel the man was beyond hope, only to see him finally be completely set free and become a successful evangelist for twenty years.

The danger is compounded by the fact that secular counselors will not point to God's grace, but will resort to humanistic therapies, most of which are completely alien to the Christian faith in their presuppositions. This is true concerning the doctrine of man and the nature of the problems that persons experience. Even Christian counselors too often operate within a secular frame of reference and using secular constructs and therapies, not even aware (in many cases) of the deep gulf between their private religious assumptions and their professional practices.

Martin Bobgan's warning therefore is timely. However, the occasional use of specialists does not need to result in the denigration of God's grace. God does not always choose to heal sickness directly, but often through medical science. The Christian thanks God and the doctor both. Real mental illness, clinically diagnosed, is but a form of physical illness. As God does not always heal an appendix but allows the surgeon to remove it, so He does not always heal the mind but blesses the efforts of those trained to treat it. Which the pastor is not. Mental illness may require prescribed medication, shock treatment, even hospital care—all of which is beyond either the pastor's knowledge or authority.

Admittedly there is a fine line here. People are emotionally ill with memories, resentments, phobias from childhood, emotional scars from abuse, all of which may if unchecked reach the stage of full-blown mental and/or physical illness, and need medical help. Yet some pastors have acquired skill in helping people find God in the healing of their memories and emotions before that medically acute stage is reached.

Where then can the line be drawn? Perhaps we can say that the pastor needs to ask himself, "Is this problem essentially physical and mental, with moral overtones; or is the problem essentially moral and spiritual with physical side-effects? What is the real root?" Problems—or even resultant aspects of them—that are clearly physical (body or mind) and that have been prayed for but remain unhealed will need the assistance of the medical profession (physicians, psychiatrists). Problems that are primarily spiritual need the pastor. Problems that are mixed may linger after the spiritual issues are settled. This is especially true with domestic entanglements and emotional excesses that have become neurotic. In these cases let the pastor pray these persons through to God, then exercise his best judgment in deciding if they should also be referred to Christian counselors who can carry them further, thus relieving the pastor of getting too deeply mired in situations too closely involving the health of his church.

COUNSELING SEX OFFENDERS

The premise of the gospel is that God's specialty through Christ is the cure of moral illnesses. Chronic sexual aberrations, such as child abuse, are moral problems. This is true even though certain weaknesses may have overtones of chemical imbalance, environment, or even inheritance. Therefore, more than one kind of physician or counselor may be needed in a team effort. But the pastor keeps in mind that the medical world can go only so far with a moral problem. By careful treatment certain compulsions may be modified, but the root problem, which is sin, is beyond either drugs or psychiatry. Weaknesses or sicknesses that involve one in evil acts require the grace of God. The sins need to be confessed in full acknowledgment of personal accountability, and forgiven by God. Teaching such persons to "forgive themselves" won't do. They have no right to forgive themselves; their only right is to accept God's forgiveness, which is always available on gospel terms.

It must forever be insisted that the real answer to the problems of child abuse, wife abuse, incest, and homosexuality is the grace of God. The pastor must be a believer in that grace. There is no such sin that is beyond the power of God's grace. The God who can heal alcoholics and deliver from nicotine addiction can prove sufficient for sexual perversions. Let the pastor keep affirming this, publicly and privately. Therefore, pastors should not denigrate the role of Christ in meeting the needs of people by a policy of referral which in effect says that in "your case Christ is *not* the answer."

A new and very sticky issue has risen in recent years respecting the pastor's relationship to sex offenders, especially child molesters and wife abusers. The state has moved into this area and has staked its claim to both jurisdiction and information. These kinds of behavior have now come to be seen as offenses against society. The arm of the law is closing in, and actions formerly frowned on are now crimes. Hence society now lays claim to the cooperation of all segments of society, including doctors and preachers. How far can a pastor shield offenders from the normal processes of the law in the name of professional privilege, without in effect becoming guilty of obstruction of justice?

Quite often offenders confess to pastors. If they are honestly seeking the kind of help the pastor is there to give—God's grace—then let the pastor work with them confidentially for a time. But he should not forget that his success in helping them will be predicated on thorough repentance on their part, which means not only straightening up but doing their own confessing to the proper persons, perhaps even to the proper agencies. Sooner or later the offender must accept responsibility and face accountability. One of the pastor's chief contributions may prove to be his skill in persuading the offender to face the music in this way.

The problem is that occasionally the pastor presumes, because of tears and emotional scenes, that a person is now clean, only to find that the perverted behavior goes on. How long is he under obligation to shield an offender from the law when more is at stake than his professional relationship with the offender, when at stake also are the bodies and perhaps even lives of the victims? When also his relationship to the state as a citizen and a responsible official is at stake?

I think we are bound to acknowledge that the right of pastors to remain silent has its limits. If the victims themselves—especially a wife—are working with the pastor in seeking to help the offender and pleading for patience, some degree of continuing counseling that remains confidential may be justified. But there may come a time when a pastor has little alternative but to say to an offender, "I cannot continue to shield you if this behavior is not stopped at once so completely that everyone involved knows it has stopped. My options are to refer you to a professional sex therapist or report you to the proper authorities."

Where are we now in this vexed question of referral? The subject is still the peril of ministers attempting counseling in areas that should be off limits to them. But we have also seen the danger of surrendering to the wolves of secularism problems that are amenable to the grace of God. We have seen the folly of pastors down-grading the power of Christ in meeting the profound needs of human beings. Yet we recognize that some problems are not essentially moral and spiritual in nature. While such problems need to be brought to the Lord in prayer, seeking His touch and guidance, they may not fall within the province of salvation and sanctification, but may be more centrally in the province of medical science, including psychiatry and psychology. When such is the case the pastor should refer, without hesitation—but doing his best, always, to steer people to Christian physicians, psychiatrists, and counselors.

In addition, certain special signs might signal the pastor that it is time to start the referral process. Suicidal talk is one—unless it is obviously spiritual and the pastor can pray the person through to God and total release on the spot. Signs of violence also are red lights. And, as has just been conceded, such abnormal overt behavior as wife or child abuse, or child molestation, may also need to be referred when the pastor's attempts are proving futile and risky. Finally, no matter what the problem is, when the pastor's counseling has reached an impasse and all further progress seems to be blocked, the pastor had better find a graceful way to extricate himself. Maybe a new therapist can find the right key.[2]

THE TRAP OF SEX COUNSELING

A wise pastoral counselor will do his best to steer clear of counseling in matters of sex. I am referring now not to the problems of the sex offender, discussed above, but to common problems of a sexual nature which are pervasive in modern society—including the church.

Many pastors, especially beginners and middle-aged, seem highly vulnerable to the subtle allure of sex counseling. Playing with fire, they sooner or later will get burned. Several factors enter in here.

First, because pastoral, the sessions are informal and unprotected by the limits that would prevail in a truly professional situation, such as fees, time limits, methods of involving spouses, the keeping of strict records, and the absence of frequent social contacts between sessions. In contrast, out of goodwill, many pastors tend to permit sessions to become (a) too long, (b) too private, and (c) too frequent.

A *second* factor is the biological spark which always exists between the sexes, which needs only an unregulated intimacy to become a flaming temptation; but on a truly professional level is restrained by guarded settings and strict objectivity.

A *third* factor, suggested already, is the extensive relationship that the pastor may already have in almost day-by-day church activities with a particular counselee, which throws them together to a dangerous and unhealthy degree. Perhaps the counselee is his secretary; or perhaps she shares services with him week after week as music director or organist; or holds an office that throws them together frequently in church administration.

A *fourth* factor is the incredible naïveté that some men have about women. They seem unaware that while the majority of the women likely to come to them are persons of pure motives in their quest for counsel and of strong character, some women are good but vulnerable. In addition, many weak women revel in masculine attention—especially if it can be a preacher; and unfortunately, downright evil women will stoop to anything to entrap a preacher.

Put these factors together and we have a deadly mix, which means that the pastor who would presume to be a sex counselor is the world's champion nitwit. As far too many have learned too late, to their everlasting shame and sorrow.

It needs to be added, however, that emotional entanglements between pastors and female counselees are not always the outgrowth of talking about sex. The specific subject of sex, as such, may never have been mentioned. But the undisciplined openness has been present, with its camaraderie and its growing excitement. They have a lot in common, sense a psychic affinity, have feelings of admiration and respect for each other, which at a restrained level may be innocent, even wholesome. But if no professional safeguards have been put in place, nothing prevents their mutual feeling from growing until suddenly they find themselves caught in a whirlpool of emotion, the kind that tends to stupefy every moral sense, including concern for consequences.

SOME SPECIAL SAFEGUARDS

What are some of the safeguards with which a wise pastor will surround himself?

1. *The grace of God, first.* But this is a sanctifying grace, which builds in him—

   a. A profound love for God that has a horror of dishonoring Him;
   b. A deep love for his wife and children, because of which he would rather die than hurt them;
   c. A profound sense of responsibility to his church and to his influence, with a keen awareness of the far-ranging, devastating effect of his sin on those who have believed in him;
   d. A highly developed ethical sense that perceives the supreme depravity of betrayal of trust;
   e. A pattern of disciplined living that builds into one's character strong resistance to temptation. (This resistance includes the habitual control of one's impulses.)

Any pastor, being human, may find himself in situations where he is aware of the development of vagrant feelings. But if he is living close to God and is aware of the checks of the Spirit, he will fight these feelings with resolute rejection and abhorrence. In time the feelings will subside.

The truth is that the Spirit is faithful, and no ministerial fall has ever occurred without the minister persisting past warning bells and red lights and roadblocks. But such headstrong plunging suggests a backsliding heart. A sanctified man who is prayed up and spiritually sensitive will tend to shrink back in holy terror. "Flee youthful lusts," Paul says to Timothy (2 Tim. 2:22). (And mid-life lusts too).

2. *In cooperation with his conscience and the Holy Spirit the wise pastor will have other safeguards in place.* First, his

wife. He should counsel with her about female counselees, even if necessary about his feelings. And listen to her. Most wives have a sixth sense about other women and about dangerous situations. A man who scorns his wife's warnings is already on the downhill slide. Furthermore, she should be brought into the counseling process if possible. Of course this assumes a counselee's confidence in the pastor's wife's discretion. Unfortunately in a few cases counselees have good reason for not wanting to include her. But if the matter is that delicate, let her go to a professional counselor with her problem and leave the pastor alone. Many "problems" would very quickly vanish if the person faced $80 or $90 fees for every hour.

3. *Furthermore, the setting should be protective.* No pastor should attempt to counsel women in a church building when no one else is around. Counseling room doors should have windows, or doors should remain ajar, or a secretary should be stationed near at hand who feels free to rap at the door with a message at any time. This kind of a setting, rigidly adhered to, would forestall many unprofessional liaisons.

4. *There should be strict time limits.* If an interview is scheduled, make it for a specific time, which the counselee understands. The secretary should be primed to announce the next counselee or obligation when the time is up; that protects the pastor from a dawdling tearful session that could go on and on. I knew of one young pastor who boasted of his three-hour counseling sessions. He was sincere but naïve and foolish.

5. *Let the pastor refuse to be overwhelmed by sympathy into agreeing to frequent sessions or secret trysts and irregular times or irregular places.* It should be a rule not to go to the woman's home unless either her husband is present or the pastor's wife accompanies him. One young pastor received a telephone plea to come at once to see the young tearful thing, a plea to which he foolishly responded.

When he got there and entered the house, she threw back her robe to display her naked body. Since they already "liked" each other fairly well, the outcome was well-nigh predictable—resulting in the loss of a man's good name, his ministry, and his family, including a crushed wife and three bewildered children. Just to read or hear about such calamities should strike holy fear into the heart of any honest pastor, a fear which in itself is a strong safeguard. Such a fear should be deliberately nurtured.

Thus far we have discussed pastoral counseling as if women would be the pastor's only counselees. This of course is not the case. Men will come and certainly some couples. But the vast majority who seek special sessions with the pastor will be women. They are more sensitive to the problems, more profoundly affected emotionally, and generally more willing to humble themselves in seeking help. It is much harder for the masculine ego to admit a need or submit to the counseling process.

There have been far too many moral tragedies among clergy. The situation is completely intolerable. Let the pastor who does not want to be another statistic cultivate the art of being scared. Let him pray God to help him be a modern Joseph who says, "How can I do such a wicked thing and sin against God?" And the church. And the clergy. And his family. And his young people. And his brothers and sisters. And his denomination. And his community. And society—which expects better things of ministers and knows how to trample underfoot the salt which has lost its moral integrity (Matt. 5:13). But far worse: every ministerial fall is a recrucifixion of Jesus and a shameful blot on the name of God.[3]

17

PASTORAL COUNSELING: ITS PRACTICE

The practice of counseling is both a science and an art, which has been for many years the subject of an enormous literature. There will be no attempt here to summarize the many different therapies or to introduce technical intricacies, which can be learned in textbooks. The desire in this chapter is to be practical and sensible. Possibly the very simplicity of a practical approach may at times have been missed in the more scholarly works. Also, it is the intention in this chapter to relate counseling to Wesleyanism and to preaching.

THE COUNSELEE'S APPROACH

Generally a first interview takes one of four forms:

1. *A request for advice about a contemplated course of action.* Often behind the request is a mind already made up. What is really wanted is confirmation—which the pastor dare not give unless he can do so conscientiously. Or the request may express an honest uncertainty. The pastor can help the person see the issues that he has subconsciously hidden from himself. The approach can be

to help the counselee himself answer the questions: Is this course of action right? Is it providential? Is it reasonable? Is the counselee prompted by a feeling of "ought," or troubled by a feeling of "ought not," or perhaps by a more neutral feeling of doubt? Has he/she talked it over with his/her spouse or with other significant or involved persons? Generally in the end the counselee can be helped to provide his own answer, though at times directive counseling is the pastor's prerogative and duty.

2. *A request for a discussion about a doctrinal question.* The person may be combative. A pastor does not need to waste much time on crusaders who have come with the firm intention of setting the pastor straight doctrinally. Only teachable counselees can be helped. "But foolish and unlearned questions avoid, knowing that they do gender strifes. And the servant of the Lord must not strive; but be gentle unto all men, apt to teach, patient, in meekness instructing those that oppose themselves" (2 Tim. 2:23–25, KJV).

At times, however, an argumentative approach is a smokescreen for a deep uncertainty, and the argumentative wall soon crumbles. The challenge to the pastor is to be sufficiently knowledgeable to be able to discuss the issue and answer the questions competently. If he displays ignorance combined with impatience, he will forfeit his opportunity. However, the ignorance combined with humility may become a learning experience for both of them. If the pastor does not know the answer, let him say so but suggest studying it out together or ask the person to give him time to research the matter. He should never belittle a question or embarrass the questioner.

3. *A request for help in sorting out a personal spiritual or ethical problem.* Why do holiness folk take certain ethical stands? When does temptation become sin? Do sanctified people ever feel angry? How can I really forgive the one

who so viciously wronged me? How should I conduct myself toward him? Does forgiveness really mean *forgetting*? How can we tithe when we owe so many people? Why is prayer so difficult for me? How can I learn to control my thoughts? Does spiritual victory mean that I will always be feeling "high" in the Lord? What does it mean to "surrender fully" to the Lord? Didn't I do that when I was converted? I believe I have the Spirit. What is different about being "filled" with the Spirit? If the pastor is sufficiently mature and secure in his own soul, he can draw help for these inquirers not only from the Bible but from his own experience.

4. *An exploratory discussion concerning a situational problem that baffles.* It may be domestic, physical, financial, interpersonal. It seems complicated and sticky or the person wouldn't be coming to the preacher to talk about it. The pastor will soon learn that most problems arise not necessarily out of carnality but out of humanity—sheer finiteness, limited knowledge, limited strength, limited wisdom. They are coping problems. Such problems need to be faced prayerfully and helpfully before they develop into full-blown illnesses, on the one hand, or, on the other, into a break with God. Sin may not be in the picture at the beginning stages of a problem, but may creep in if it is allowed to go unsolved and uncontrolled. The sin may be in the form of compromising solutions, unkind words and actions, or a drift into resentments, ruptures, and bitterness.

AN APPROPRIATE METHODOLOGY

Such are the basic types of request. In defining them, appropriate pastoral responses have in some cases already been indicated. But can more be said about a common methodology suitable for all of them? What should a pastor be endeavoring to do?

1. *Help the person or persons unwrap the problem.* The real problem may be hidden in many thicknesses of irrelevant and extraneous issues. But if the pastor will patiently listen and refrain from snap judgments and subjective responses, the core matter will emerge. Getting to the bottom of a situation may take more than one session. But until the bottom is reached any pastoral counsel is premature. Without being rejecting or judgmental, the pastor can adroitly and gently ask the leading questions that will unfold realities layer by layer.

2. *Help the counselee put the problem in perspective.* For one thing, he or she must see where it stands in relation to a mature and Christian value system. Is the problem being blown out of proportion to its real importance? Or, more seriously, perhaps a clear-eyed perception of the unnoticed moral issues may be needed.

3. *Help the counselee see the problem from the standpoint of the other persons who may be involved.* This will be difficult because at first counselees tend to be blind to any viewpoint other than their own. They are aware of their own feelings, their own rights (and perhaps their violation), their own happiness. In many cases if these persons can be helped to transpose themselves into the other person's skin, and try to understand where he or she is coming from and what his or her feelings are, the mood will soften and the solution will be well within reach.

4. *Help the counselee find God's solution.* This, of course, should always, undeviatingly, be the objective of a Christian pastor. He should forever be reminding the counselee of certain basic axioms. One, God is interested in every problem and has a solution for every problem. Two, God's answer or course of action is always the right one, always best for everyone concerned, and always the

route to the greatest possible happiness in the long run. These claims express the faith of a Christian. If a pastor is not strengthening this faith and fostering the spiritual-mindedness which learns to look for God's answer, he is missing his pastoral role.

Of course he may discover before he has gone far that God's will is not what the counselee really wants. He wants his own. He wants to be vindicated. He wants the matter set right according to his own idea of what that should be. Making the matter an earnest and honest subject of prayer does not appeal to him. He is actually afraid of proceeding in that direction, for he is afraid of what God may say. He might have to bend his will. He might have to be willing to see that perhaps he or she is (at least partially) in the wrong. God may demand that he or she do the changing, whereas the counselee has clung to the insistence that the other person do the changing. He may have to forgive and he is not willing to forgive.

God's will may be more grace rather than deliverance from the thorn, as was the case with Paul (2 Cor. 12:7–9). This solution may best glorify God but it may not suit the counselee at all. He doesn't want to settle for more grace; he wants nothing short of a miracle of deliverance from his circumstance.

If a pastor discovers this roadblock, he must deal with it faithfully. As far as he is concerned, this is now the real problem. The matter about which the counselee came to talk has become secondary. For the pastor's attempts to counsel will prove abortive if he proceeds to help the counselee find a solution that is not God's. This would be a betrayal of both God and the counselee. As a Christian he knows that any solution that seeks to make an end run around God is no solution at all. The consequences can be only ultimately disastrous.

Therefore, the pastor must deal with the counselee's

own soul. He must help him or her see that aversion to the spiritual and biblical answer is sin. Involved are the sins of pride, rebellion, and unbelief. Persistence in such sin cannot but block God's remedial action, and open the door wide to the delusions of Satan and the darkness of the hardened heart. Instead of being resolved, the situation originally brought to the pastor will only deteriorate until in time it will reach the point of no return.

No pastor can help along these lines unless he is thoroughly familiar with the Bible. It won't do to ignore the Bible in favor of contemporary authorities. While the specific problem may not be named in the Bible, the Bible will contain principles which clearly and definitely bear on it. The open Bible should be prominent on the pastor's desk, from the start of the interview. Any pastor who feels that bringing religion into the session so overtly and immediately is somehow gauche or beneath his professional dignity needs to be converted. Of course if he is better acquainted with the latest textbook than with the Bible he may flounder in trying to use the Bible in a counseling session.

It bears repeating that any recommendation or proposed solution that does not reach the moral and religious dimension as illuminated in the Scriptures is bound to be shallow and merely utilitarian. And the counselee who is impatient with the moral and theological issues of his problem and would brush them aside will never have the right answer.

The pastor can always operate in dependence on the Holy Spirit, knowing that the Spirit is faithful to illuminate the mind and clarify the conscience. If the counselee is not a Christian, the pastor may be sure that right there, as the counselee sits in front of him, the Spirit is convicting him of personal need and projecting before his view the moral and spiritual ramifications of his problem.

The pastor should be so confident of this that he will feel free gently to direct the whole discussion to the issue of salvation. To fail to do so would be as negligent as for a doctor to let a patient who came to him about his sniffles get away with nothing being said about the cancerous growth on his face.

If the counselee is a Christian, then one may be sure that the Holy Spirit is on duty and that beneath the quizzing, quibbling, and bewilderment He is gently prodding in a certain direction. The pastor's task will be to help the Christian recognize and acknowledge what the Spirit is saying. Then the matter won't hang on the pastor's wisdom after all.

COUNSELING AND WESLEYANISM

Can the Wesleyan pastor's special obligations be delineated in even greater detail? Let us try. Fundamentally, the pastor should hold his counselees, whether members of his church or not, to the biblical standard of holiness. This is not a standard invented by the Holiness Movement or by John Wesley. The pastor should never concede for one moment anything less than the revealed plan of God, which is "to be holy" (Eph. 1:4).

This includes holding counselees

—to the demand for total consecration and obedience.
—to the biblical norms of marriage, family, sex, and divorce.
—to the biblical norms of stewardship and vocation.
—to the biblical norms of love and forgiveness.

But in this last respect the failure of the contemporary models of pastoral care must be carefully avoided, namely, an emphasis on love that loosens moral demands.

Martin Marty observes that never have there been more evangelicals but less impact on the moral life of the nation. What is the explanation? Two factors: the twisted interpretation of "grace alone" so prevalent today—that eternal salvation in no sense depends on personal obedience and righteousness, but only on a once-for-all new birth, the benefits of which are nonforfeitable, no matter what subsequent sinning may occur. The second factor is the almost universal softness about love and forgiveness, which forgets that there can be neither without repentance. The sign, "Not better, only forgiven," is symptomatic. Scandals involving TV and other ministries are the most glaring eruption of the moral consequence both in religion and the nation. The pastor therefore who softens the moral fiber of his people by constantly harping on God's *unconditional* love, without explanation or qualification, is guilty of malpractice.[1]

ADJUNCT HELPS

The pastor who loves his people and seeks to help them in every possible way will not hesitate to multiply his own efforts by the use of whatever Christian adjunct helps are available.

These helps include carefully structured Marriage Enrichment Retreats, provided the couples leading the sessions are certified and really know what they are about. Films such as the two series by James Dobson are helpful in some settings. In the pastor's study should be a supply of pertinent booklets that deal with today's problems (from a sound evangelical and Wesleyan standpoint). When the counselee leaves the study, one of these could wisely be put into his or her hand. As was urged in a previous chapter, books on holiness should be kept constantly before the people.

And not incidentally (though it may appear so here), there are limits to which a pastor should allow himself to get involved with family financial problems. Remember what Jesus said to the brother who called on Jesus to compel a fair distribution of the estate. The Lord replied, "Who made me a ruler and a judge over you?" Not a bad motto to have on one's desk—facing the counselee.

In all of these human relationships the pastor needs wit, warmth, and wisdom. Sometimes the best elixir for a tight situation is a good laugh. When a board member came storming up to the parsonage with the hot accusation, "Down at the barbershop just now Brother Jones called me a skunk! What are you going to do about it?" the pastor, W. E. Cox, just smiled and said, "If you don't make a stink about it no one will believe him." The man said nothing more. Laughter is healthful for a lot of situations, if the pastor can only help people see the funny side of their problems, and learn to laugh at themselves.

If pleasantries fail to soften some hardhead, certain passages of Scripture could be read to him, such as "The wisdom that is from above is first pure, then peaceable, gentle, and easy to be entreated" (James 3:17, KJV). Bear down on the implication. A wise person is reasonable. You can talk to him. He is not rigid and intractable. Sometimes to begin with such a Bible passage and then have prayer will be sufficient to quench some of the fire and prompt a receptive and humble frame of mind.

COUNSELING AND PREACHING

One final but vital question must be raised. *What should be the relation of the pastor's counseling to his preaching?*

The counseling should match the preaching. It is folly for one to preach the gospel in the pulpit and then bring secular, humanistic, and Pelagian concepts into the counseling room. Does he preach that people are sinners and need to repent and believe on Christ as Savior? that believers need to be sanctified wholly and filled with the Spirit? that Christians are expected to live lives of prayer, righteousness, and good works? that Christians need to "grow in grace and in the knowledge of the Lord Jesus Christ"? that Christians should be forgiving, loving, patient and kind, producing increasingly the fruit of the Spirit? that holiness is more important than happiness? that getting to heaven is more important than making money? Then let him bring these truths into the counseling room. If they are true in one place, they are true in another. If these are needed by the crowd on Sunday morning, they are needed by the individual on Tuesday morning in the study. These are the same people—or at least people like them.

Let the pastor read again the survey in chapter fifteen of the kinds of problems likely to arise. Does his Sunday preaching have no bearing on these? Then it is to be feared that in the pulpit he is irrelevant. But if his preaching reaches the human situation—if it bears on the everyday problems and needs of human beings—the ground will already have been laid for the counseling session during the week. Let the pastor apply what he has preached to this particular situation. If it was on the mark on Sunday it will be also on the mark on Wednesday. The counseling session, whether in the counselee's home or in the pastor's study or in the vestibule after church or on the street corner, will provide a golden opportunity to reinforce the pastor's sermons by their judicious application to one particular person at one special point in his life.

18

THE POWER OF THE PASTOR

The September 21, 1986, edition of the *Washington Post* published a remarkable statement of Franklin D. Roosevelt: "No greater thing could come to our land today than a revival of the spirit of religion—a revival that would sweep through the homes of the nation and stir the hearts of men and women of all faiths to a reassertion of their belief in God and their dedication to His will for themselves and for their world. I doubt if there is any problem—social, political or economic—that would not melt away before the fire of such a spiritual awakening."[1]

This is an eloquent confession that the state is powerless to do what most needs to be done. For the state cannot promote such a revival actively and directly. This is the role of the church, and Roosevelt's statement testifies to the cruciality of this role and the enormous responsibility of the church. He understood as clearly as anyone the futility of the political process in fashioning a righteous society. Government can protect freedoms and regulate external conduct in certain limited areas, but government is powerless to make men and women holy. Only Christ can do that; and the church, not the state, is

God's instrument in channeling Christ's redemptive grace. Therefore the hope of the state lies in the success of the church. When the church fails, society rapidly disintegrates and the state is powerless to prevent it.

The perennial credo of the liberal and humanist is that education can adequately complement the state in the formation of a strong society. But as our investment in education climbs so does crime and immorality and lawlessness. Obviously, education without a moral and religious base can only sharpen the wits of thugs and thieves.

Roosevelt is just one of many world leaders who have declared the primacy of the spiritual dimension of life and the impotence of law apart from goodwill. Arnold Toynbee, Charles Lindbergh, Dag Hammarskjöld, Douglas MacArthur, and Ronald Reagan have all made similar solemn pronouncements.

In May 1988, Prime Minister Margaret Thatcher spoke to the General Assembly of the Church of Scotland. She said:

> The truths of the Judaic-Christian tradition are infinitely precious, not only, as I believe, because they are true, but also because they provide the moral impulse which alone can lead to that peace . . . for which we all long . . . There is little hope for democracy if the hearts of men and women . . . cannot be touched by a call to something greater than themselves. Political structures, state institutions, collective ideals are not enough. We parliamentarians can legislate for the rule of law. You the church can teach the life of faith.[2]

Roosevelt, Mrs. Thatcher, and all perceptive statesmen understand what churchmen have too often strangely forgotten: that the church is at the vanguard of all social progress. The church is the stabilizing force that keeps society from slipping into anarchy. As the body of Christ, the church is God's appointed means of transmitting truth and grace to the souls of people and thereby transforming them. When the church fails, the cults rush into the vacuum.

When that wondrous revival swept across the prairies of Canada in 1972, entire communities were cleansed. Comments were made by the city fathers of Saskatoon that the city was so transformed that they could almost dismiss their police force. Businessmen were heartened by the wave of restitution. Wrongs were confessed, stolen goods returned, long-neglected debts paid. Shattered families were put back together. Shaky families were grounded on the Rock. The drug grip was broken in the lives of many. These are the things which all thoughtful people in our day realize need to be done; yet they stand helpless when searching for ways to accomplish these ends by humanistic means. The Christian knows that all forms of humanism are vain hopes, and that only the church has the answer.

It becomes clear therefore that in the scale of importance the pastor ranks higher than the politician, for the pastor's work makes the politician's success possible. The pastor works with people at the character level, and without good character in its citizenry no democracy can survive. While the minister of the gospel belongs first of all to Christ, and while his primary purpose is not to promote his nation but the kingdom of Christ, it is nevertheless true that as a correlative obligation he is also the servant of "Caesar"—indeed, Caesar's best hope. The pastor's success is more crucial to the well-being of a nation than armaments.

Therefore, the greatest need of this generation is an army of God-called, Spirit-filled pastors who can lead their churches in such a way that the spiritual awakening and rebirth identified as our need by Roosevelt can occur. Instead of permitting themselves to be intimidated by the imposing world around of doctors, lawyers, and politicians, pastors should throw back their shoulders and stand tall with a sense of incalculable power and immeasurable responsibility. This awareness must not be confused with pride or be permitted to foster pride; certainly not self-reliance. Rather, this awareness should be profoundly grounded in a biblical worldview and a personal mandate from God Himself.

But if the church is going to be effective in this day, the caliber of its pastors must be very high. They need to be giants intellectually and spiritually. Pygmies will not do. These are days when mediocrity in the ministry is simply not acceptable. Some of us are limited in our native abilities, but this does not have to mean mediocrity. Men and women of average abilities can become towers of strength and giants of effectiveness. What is needed is not greater brilliance but greater depth; not flashier schemes but deeper devotion; not more money but more prayer; not more cleverness but more holiness.

What is needed is a greater measure of the Holy Spirit's power in a pastor's heart and on his ministry.

We need pastors, men and women, who magnify their calling. Who stand tall as lights in their communities, showing men and women by their steadfast patience, their loving service, and their totally reliable pattern of shepherding year in and year out that not only is the church the body of Christ but that it is society's beacon and humanity's only hope.

NOTES

Chapter 1
Our Perspective—From Above or From Below?

[1] This is not a license to be slipshod in keeping records such as membership roll, attendance records, or finances. A pastor can be meticulous in such details yet enjoy the inner rest of knowing that their real interpretation and evaluation is beyond the province of people.

Chapter 2
Theological Foundations

[1] As demonstrated in the Hebrides Revival of 1949–51, when in one case some 600 people gathered outside a church at 11 p.m., not knowing why they were there, and in another village hundreds were awakened and drawn to the church at 4 a.m. Similar divine power was manifested in the revival that swept Western Canada in 1972.

[2] We will do well to heed the words of David F. Wells: "The simple point that has to be rediscovered and should never have been lost is that the Spirit's power comes only in conjuntion with his work of truth and holiness. Our obsession with his power is really an obsession with results." He further points out that power detached from truth and holiness "bears more resemblance to that of Satan than to that of the Holy Spirit." *God the Evangelist: How the Holy Spirit Works to Bring Men and Women to Faith* (Grand Rapids: Eerdmans, 1987), 94.

Chapter 5
The Pastor As Instrument

[1] Harry R. Boer, *Pentecost and Missions* (Grand Rapids: Eerdmans, 1961), 31.

[2] A Roman province in what is now northwestern Turkey.

[3] E. M. Bounds, *Power Through Prayer* (Grand Rapids, Baker, n.d.), 5.

Chapter 6
Some Parameters of Church Growth

[1] *Journal of the Evangelical Theological Society* 30, no. 4 (Dec. 1987): 473. J. I. Packer, in his Introduction to *God the Evangelist,* observes: "Suffering is the Christian's road home; no other road leads us there. But the twentieth-century West has come to think of a life free from pain and trouble as virtually a natural human right, and Christian minds have been so swamped by this thinking that nowadays any pain and loss in a Christian's life is felt to cast doubt on God's goodness. It is perhaps no wonder that our age has produced the gospel of health and wealth, promising that God will give us right now whatever we name and claim under either heading; no wonder, either, that the triumphs of the 'power encounter' between the Christ of the gospels and the secular and satanic forces . . . should be equated by some with supernatural healings of the physical body rather than with supernatural transformations of the moral character" (p. xv).

[2] Stacy Rinehart and Paula Rinehart, *Living in Light of Eternity,* (Colorado Springs: NAVPRESS, 1986), 118.

[3] As Bill Burch says, "Sanctification builds some inside braces."

Chapter 7
Reaching People—Ways That Work

[1] More will be said about "purposeful contacts" in chapter eight. Perhaps it should be noted here that while all contacts should be purposeful in the broadest sense, it is not necessary to think of every visit with a family or person as an occasion for immediate evangelizing.

Contacts that are primarily social often prepare the way for more serious subjects later. Pastors who know how to enter into the interests and enthusiasms of people will be the pastors who will later be allowed into the inner rooms of life. Bishop William A. Quayle many years ago said, "You may not have the cattle trader's instinct; but if that person enjoys cattle you can enjoy them because he does. . . . This ability to transfer viewpoints and so enjoy what others enjoy because they enjoy it, is the finest possible test of the fineness of culture." *The Pastor–Preacher* (New York: The Methodist Book Concern, 1915), 177.

Chapter 8
Drawing the Net

[1] Every church needs a sanctified spark plug. It doesn't have to be the pastor, but there should be at least one vibrant, magnetic personality who can inspire enthusiasm, action, and loyalty.

Chapter 9
Systems of Acceleration

[1] "Of all the nuisances to plague us over the years," writes one irate housewife to Abigail Van Buren, "telemarketing is at the top of the list." She calls it a "blatant invasion of privacy." While some pastors are exclaiming that "The Phone's For You" system is a God-send, one wonders if for every friendly response there may not be a dozen who will fume against the church that uses the method. It is risky to make a few friends at the expense of making many enemies. Just a thought.

Chapter 10
The Revival Campaign

[1] An account of the revival and of the author's blessing from it was written by Shirwood Wirt in *Afterglow: The Excitement of Being Filled With the Spirit* (Grand Rapids: Zondervan, 1975).

[2] Evangelist Chuck Milhuff reports that when he asked the veteran pastor Robert G. Lee his opinion of revivals, the response was

unhesitating: "If churches stop holding regular, planned revivals they will lose their redemptive purpose in the world." He was then in his eighties and holding a revival in Clovis, New Mexico.

Chapter 11
Growing Sturdy Saints

[1] Editorial, "The Truth is—There's Plenty of Conflict to Manage," *The Preacher's Magazine,* 64, no. 3 (March/April/May 1989): 1.

[2] Robert W. Zinnecker's counsel is wise: "In its rush for new members or expanded programs, the church has occasionally given leadership roles to persons who have caused many problems and brought little success. We must have the discipline to encourage a feeling of responsibility for our church's forward movement while assuring that the basic truths of our faith are not altered in their presentation. We can't compromise our faith by giving leadership roles to those who do not share our basic doctrines and beliefs." "In Search of Excellent Churches," *The Sounding Board* 5, no. 2 (Spring 1987): 15.

Chapter 12
The Dynamics of Growth

[1] *The Christian Mind,* by Harry Blamires (Ann Arbor: Servant, 1978) is written against the background of a British culture and even particularly a Church of England setting, but still is very helpful in aiding a mature reader in understanding in practical terms what it means to think like a Christian.

[2] A pastor would do well to become thoroughly familiar with the rich material in H. Orton Wiley's *Christian Theology,* vol. 3, pp. 24–67, and use this in suitable forms in his task of Christian nurturing.

[3] Or depression. The majority of depressions are self-induced, and often begin at the point of some small crisis in which the Christian takes a wrong attitude or fails to obey. Instead of committing the hurt or reversal to the Lord or instead of courageously facing God's new signals, the person begins to brood or become stubborn. Then withdrawal follows and depression sets in. Since its cause is spiritual, its cure will be also.

⁴A. Skevington Wood, *The Burning Heart* (Grand Rapids: Eerdmans, 1967), 191.

Chapter 13
Shepherding Toward Heart Holiness

¹A recent helpful book is Keith W. Drury, *Holiness for Ordinary People* (Grand Rapids: Zondervan/Francis Asbury Press, 1987). A much more comprehensive volume, which should be in every home, is *Holiness Teaching Today,* vol. 6 of *Great Holiness Classics,* Albert F. Harper, ed. (Kansas City: Beacon Hill, 1987). For other titles, see Selected Bibliography.

²Obviously this is a Wesleyan/Arminian statement. Others would express some of these concepts differently.

³This does not mean that we must confine ourselves to the stately hymns. Many fine choruses are substantive as well as inspiring. People enjoy singing choruses, and should not be deprived of this pleasure. But church music needs to have a balance and include a large amount of formative doctrinal content.

⁴A textbook dealing solely with holiness preaching as a unique homiletical and doctrinal genre, having its own special principles and rules, is available in Richard S. Taylor, *Preaching Holiness Today,* rev. ed. (Kansas City: Beacon Hill, 1987).

⁵"The Devil's Electric Carrot," *Christianity Today* 17, no. 4 (February 16, 1973): 18.

Chapter 14
Some Crucial Areas of Nurture

¹R. Duane Thompson, "In the Wesleyan Spirit: A Study in Wesleyan Spirituality," *The Preacher's Magazine* 64, no. 3 (March/April/May 1989): 43.

²David F. Wells says: "It is one of the ironies of modern evangelicalism that while it has upheld the biblical doctrine of sin, it has largely succeeded in eliminating the biblical doctrine of worldliness." He explains that we have so reacted against the extreme emphasis on externals as marks of worldliness that as a result we have come to the

place where we have "no sense of worldliness at all" (*God the Evangelist,* 97).

Chapter 15
Pastoral Counseling—Its Uniqueness

[1] Don S. Browning, *The Moral Context of Pastoral Care* (Philadelphia: Westminster, 1976), 12.

[2] Ibid., p. 15.

[3] Ibid.

[4] Jacob Firet *The Moral Context,* tr. John Vriend (Grand Rapids: Eerdmans, 1986), 25.

[5] *Dynamics in Pastoring* (Grand Rapids: Eerdmans, 1986), 15.

Chapter 16
Pastoral Counseling—Its Perils

[1] Martin and Deidre Bobgan, *Psychoheresy: The Psychological Seduction of Christianity* (Santa Barbara, Calif.: East Gate, 1987). Similar warnings are voiced by W. Stanley Johnson, professor of theology at Western Evangelical Seminary. He urges a dialogue between theologians and psychologists. But he says, "There are risks. . . . One of the problems in interfacing that has actually occurred is the diminution of the role of Christian principles. In the field of psychology, sometimes the problems of dealing with complex personalities can undermine confidence in the soteric ministries of the Spirit of God. Another problem is that of adopting, for example, a person-centered methodology at the expense of universal and foundational truths" (Editorial, *Kardia: A Journal of Wesleyan Thought* 4, no. 1 [Spring 1989]): 6.

[2] There is danger of pastors allowing their valuable time to be leeched by a few chronic neurotics whose problems are perennial. Occasionally there is even such a person who really doesn't want solutions, only attention. As Roger C. Palms says, a small group manage to tie up ninety percent of the pastor's time. "It's a shock to some who fancy themselves heavily involved in counseling when a time study shows that their counseling is with the same few, week in

and week out, who are not really open to help." *God Guides Your Tomorrows* (Downers Grove: InterVarsity Press, 1987), 38.

[3] See Dean Merrill, "The Sexual Hazards of Pastoral Care" *Christianity Today* (November 8, 1985), 105.

Chapter 17
Pastoral Counseling—Its Practice

[1] Speaking of our contemporary tendency to be overly charitable toward moral failure, David F. Wells says: "But that pardon which we extend so easily and even with a sense of piety is a depth charge whose detonation demolishes the biblical teaching on holiness and spirituality. In accepting what should in fact be repudiated and even exposed, we are setting ourselves completely at odds with the work of the Holy Spirit. Can we continue to be baffled, then, that we do not experience his powerful blessing in our lives and our ministries?" (*God the Evangelist*, 97).

Chapter 18
The Power of the Pastor

[1] Bob Arnebeck, "FDR Invoked God, Too," *Washington Post*, September 21, 1986. Quoted in *Televangelism: Power and Politics on God's Frontiers*, by Jeffry K. Hadden and Anson Shupe (New York: Henry Holt, 1988), 272.

[2] Quoted by Charles Colson, in "A Challenge to the New President," *Jubilee* (January 1989), 7.

SELECTED BIBLIOGRAPHY

Aldrich, Joseph. *Life-Style Evangelism*. Portland, Ore.: Multnomah, 1981.

Blamire, Harry. *The Christian Mind*. Ann Arbor: Servant, 1978.

Bobgan, Martin and Deidre. *Psychoheresy: The Psychological Seduction of Christianity*. Santa Barbara, Calif.: East Gate, 1987.

Bounds, E. M. *Power Through Prayer*. Grand Rapids: Baker, n.d.

Bradshaw, Malcolm R. *Church Growth Through Evangelism in Depth*. South Pasadena, Calif.: William Carey Library, 1969.

Carter, Charles W. *From Revival to Evangelism*. Salem, Ohio: Harold E. Schmul, 1986.

Coleman, Lucien E., Jr. *Why the Church Must Teach*. Nashville: Broadman, 1984.

Coppedge, Allan. *The Biblical Principles of Discipleship*. Grand Rapids: Zondervan/Francis Asbury Press, 1989.

Duewel, Wesley L. *Ablaze for God*. Grand Rapids: Zondervan/Francis Asbury Press, 1989.

Dunnam, Maxie. *Alive in Christ: The Dynamic Process of Spiritual Formation*. Nashville: Abingdon, 1982.

Ellul, Jacques. *The Subversion of Christianity*. Grand Rapids: Eerdmans, 1986.

Escott, Harry, ed. *The Cure of Souls: An Anthology of P. T. Forsyth's Practical Writings*. Grand Rapids: Eerdmans, 1971.

Firet, Jacob. *Dynamics in Pastoring*. Grand Rapids: Eerdmans, 1986.

Garlow, James L. *Partners in Ministry: Laity and Pastors Working Together*. Kansas City: Beacon Hill, 1984.

Greenway, Roger S., ed. *The Pastor-Evangelist: Preacher, Model, and Mobilizer for Church Growth*. Phillipsburg, N.J.: Presbyterian and Reformed, 1987.

Harper, Albert, ed. *Great Holiness Classics,* Vol. 6, *Holiness Teaching Today*. Kansas City: Beacon Hill, 1987.

Hurding, Roger F. *The Tree of Healing*. Grand Rapids: Zondervan, 1987.

Johnston, Jon and Bill M. Sullivan, eds. *The Smaller Church in a Super Church Era*. Kansas City: Beacon Hill, 1984.

Lawson, E. LeRoy and Tetsunao Yamamori. *Church Growth: Everybody's Business*. Cincinnati: Standard, 1973.

Maner, Robert. *Making the Small Church Grow*. Kansas City: Beacon Hill, 1984.

McGavran, Donald Anderson. *Church Growth: Strategies that Work*. Nashville: Abingdon, 1980.

————, ed. *Church Growth and Christian Mission*. San Francisco: Harper & Row, 1965.

Miller, C. John. *Outgrowing the Ingrown Church*. Grand Rapids: Zondervan, 1986.

Oden, Thomas C. *Doctrinal Standards in the Wesleyan Tradition*. Grand Rapids: Zondervan/Francis Asbury Press, 1988.

Perkins, Hal. *Leadership Multiplication* (discipling curriculum in eight paperbacks). Kansas City: Beacon Hill, 1983.

Peterson, Eugene. *Working the Angles: The Shape of Pastoral Integrity*. Grand Rapids: Eerdmans, 1987.

Rinehart, Stacy and Paula. *Living in Light of Eternity*. Colorado Springs: NavPress, 1986.

Stanger, Frank Bateman. *Spiritual Formation in the Local Church*. Zondervan/Francis Asbury Press, 1989.

Taylor, Richard S. *Preaching Holiness Today*, rev. Kansas City: Beacon Hill, 1987.

Tippett, Alan Richard. *Church Growth and the Word of God*. Grand Rapids: Eerdmans, 1970.

Wagner, C. Peter. *Church Growth and the Whole Gospel*. San Francisco: Harper & Row, 1981.

————. *Leading Your Church to Growth*. Glendale, Calif.: Regal, 1984.

Wellmon, Don. *Dynamics of Discipleship: A Curriculum on Discipleship*. Kansas City: Beacon Hill, 1984.

Wells, David F. *God the Evangelist: How the Holy Spirit Works to Bring Men and Women to Faith*. Grand Rapids: Eerdmans, 1987.

Wilson, Marlene. *How to Mobilize Church Volunteers*. Minneapolis: Augsburg, 1983.

Wirt, Sherwood. *Afterglow: The Excitement of Being Filled With the Spirit*. Grand Rapids: Zondervan, 1975.

Zuck, Roy B. *The Holy Spirit in Your Teaching*. Wheaton, Ill.: Victor, 1984.